TWENTY-TWO LESSONS FOR NOW

TWENTY-TWO LESSONS FOR NOW

A GUIDE TO CRAFTING A LIFE OF MEANING AND JOY

LESSONS
— *by* —
TREVOR WALLER

Man is a deciding being
— VIKTOR FRANKL

22 LESSONS
— by —
TREVOR WALLER

First published by Trevor Waller, 2020
Second Edition, September 2021
Third Edition, June 2022
(Previously published as "22 Lessons for Corona Time & After")

Copyright © 2022 by Trevor Waller

ISBN 978-0-620-88019-0 (e-book)
ISBN 978-0-620-88041-1 (print)

Author:
Trevor Waller (www.22lessons.com)
Editors:
Phillipa Mitchell (www.phillipamitchell.com)
Yvonne Shapiro (yvonne.t.shapiro@gmail.com)
Editorial Assistant:
David Schiffman (david.designedcontent@gmail.com)
First and Second Editions Designer:
Gregg Davies (www.greggdavies.com)
Third Edition Designer:
Bradley Kirshenbaum (www.lovejozi.com)

All rights reserved

The moral right of the author has been asserted

No part of this publication may be reproduced, distributed, or transmitted in any form or by any means, including photocopying, recording, or other electronic or mechanical methods, without the prior written permission of the author, except in the case of brief quotations embodied in critical reviews and certain other non-commercial uses permitted by copyright law.

Additional copies of this book can be purchased from all leading book retailers worldwide.

Oh, the comfort, the inexpressible comfort of feeling safe with a person; having neither to weigh thoughts nor measure words, but to pour them all out, just as they are, chaff and grain together, knowing that a faithful hand will take and sift them, keep what is worth keeping, and then, with a breath of kindness, blow the rest away.

— DINAH MARIA MULOCK CRAIK

For Dor, Debbie, Keshie, Matan and Azi,
my 'inner-inner' circle, who have taught me so
much and for Anbin, my Lesson 23.

PROLOGUE:	TWO 'PRE-LESSONS'	**1**
LESSON 1:	TRUST THE PROCESS (TTP)	**11**
LESSON 2:	MONDAY BEFORE TUESDAY	**17**
LESSON 3:	THE INFORMATION IS NEUTRAL	**23**
LESSON 4:	DON'T BE ATTACHED TO THE OUTCOME	**29**
LESSON 5:	MAKE IT UP AS YOU GO ALONG	**35**
LESSON 6:	BE GRATEFUL	**41**
LESSON 7:	PRACTISE PATIENCE	**49**
LESSON 8:	GIVE IT A NAME	**57**
LESSON 9:	WATCH THOSE EXPECTATIONS	**63**
LESSON 10:	BE REAL	**71**
LESSON 11:	TELL THE TRUTH FASTER (TTTF)	**77**
LESSON 12:	PLAY IN THE LIGHT	**83**
LESSON 13:	CHOOSE AGAIN	**91**
LESSON 14:	DECIDE WITH LOVE, NOT FEAR	**99**
LESSON 15:	READ THE SIGNS	**105**
LESSON 16:	BE KIND	**111**
LESSON 17:	SHOW UP	**119**
LESSON 18:	LOWER YOUR BUCKET	**125**
LESSON 19:	TRAVEL LIGHT	**133**
LESSON 20:	DROP THE COMPARISON	**141**
LESSON 21:	BREATHE	**149**
LESSON 22:	YAY ME!	**155**
AFTERWORD		**161**

PROLOGUE:
TWO 'PRE-LESSONS'

*Even the Ten Commandments
had a First Draft*

— DAVID BOICE

In 2018, I wrote a book called 'The Lessons'. It was written as a gift to my niece, Keshie, who was planning to travel overseas when she finished high school. It contained 22 'lessons for life' – things I had learned and that I wanted her, and, eventually, my two younger nephews to carry with them. They were lessons that I had endeavoured to teach them over the course of their lives. I had also learned some of the lessons from them. The book sat on my laptop for two years as I busied myself with earning money and growing my business. I tried, but never succeeded, to take it further.

In 2020, when South Africa went into her initial twenty-one-day lockdown, in response to Covid-19, my opportunity-seeking brain connected '21 days' and '22 lessons'. I decided to post one of these lessons on Facebook for every day of the lockdown, with a little Covid-19 'twist' added to the mix. They were far from perfect, and not all original. I have learned so much from so many wise souls: I endeavoured, wherever possible, to acknowledge and credit these teachers. As I began posting my daily missives, so my Facebook friends began responding. Some of them began sharing the posts, and I began to get friend requests from strangers and comments from friends of friends. The feedback was overwhelmingly positive and extremely encouraging. Lockdown was providing many people within my Facebook circle with time for introspection. The posts were landing and resonating. My joy at having created a daily ritual, filled with meaning and purpose, grew daily. Some days were hard, and I shared this openly.

I had long wanted to create a website, and the lockdown seemed as good a time as any to stop procrastinating. I am grateful to my friend Anton Olivier who rose to the challenge in record time. The posts became blogs, and then the blogs became the first edition of this book. I self-published the book, and printed a limited number of copies. Friends began buying it for their friends and soon their friends began asking for books. And then strangers began enquiring about where they could get copies. A school ordered 80 books for their teachers. The lessons were resonating for people. Suddenly, I needed to print additional copies.

In the period between the first and second edition, I realised that the first edition, written under the pressure of lockdown and a daily deadline, was missing two crucial lessons that actually underpin the other 22 lessons. I learned them when I was so young that I did not even consider them 'lessons'. But the story behind them is so integral to my life that, without it, the book felt like it was missing something. This is the story that has framed my life, and which I included in the second edition.

* * *

The day I was born, it snowed in Johannesburg – a city better known for dust. The unusual weather marked the beginning of a decidedly unusual childhood. I grew up in a residential hotel, managed and run by my parents, located in the 'poor white' suburb of Langlaagte. In keeping with the laws of 1970s South Africa, the hotel had a space for every conceivable class and defined race. If you were white, could pay your way and needed a place to rest, you could rent a room at The Fountains. If you were Indian or Coloured (and male), you could drink in the 'Indian Bar', whose entrance was found on the side of the hotel, away from the white bars and lounges. Unfortunately, if you were black, you could only buy your liquor from the 'non-white' side of the bottle store. If you were then desperate to get drunk, you could hide behind the big fridge while furtively downing your drink. I think many people have forgotten (or don't know) how crazy and cruel apartheid was.

As I describe in **Lesson 16 (Be Kind)**, the hotel had a large backyard where the workers could relax, away from the pressures of their taskmasters in the front. I loved the yard and would spend my afternoons doing my homework there. One afternoon, I noticed Moses staring at me. Moses was known as a 'scullery boy'. This meant that he washed the endless glasses that came from the bar. Moses was a quiet man, one of the younger of the 'boys'. I imagine that at the time, Moses must have been in his early 20s. I started to notice how he often watched me as I did my homework. That day, Moses sat closer to me and seemed to be more interested in my books than usual. I asked him if he wanted to see my reader. He smiled at me.

"I want to be a waiter," he said suddenly.

"So ask my dad," I replied.

He looked down at the floor.

"I can't read," he said.

"What do you mean, you can't read?" I asked.

I was eight years old and motoring my way through Enid Blyton books faster than my mother could buy them for me. I had never even considered the possibility of an adult not being able to read.

"I left school when I was a small boy," Moses explained. "My parents did not have money, and I had to work on my father's farm."

I didn't say anything. I looked around the yard at David, the waiter, Monica, my nanny, and the myriad other servants as they went about their duties. *Was it possible that they, too, could not read? How can you live without being able to read?* Suddenly, I looked down at my pencil, and it hit me that if they couldn't read, maybe they could not write either!

I held out my pencil to Moses. "I will teach you," I said, "I will teach you to read and write."

And so, every day after school, I would take my books into the backyard and, having completed my homework, Moses and I would sit together as I taught this twenty-something-year-old Zulu man to read and write in English. Slowly, slowly, day by day, starting with what I had been taught in Grade 1, I showed Moses how to sound out the letters, how to put them together and then how to say them. I was playing school with a real person, and I loved every minute of it! Moses and I became quite a sight as we sat on beer crates, and he slowly, painstakingly, began to read. Moses was bright, and I was determined (or maybe, it was the other way round). Either way, it took us a year. When I finished Grade 3, Moses had sufficient ability in English to ask my dad if he could be a waiter. Not long after, Moses became a waiter. And I had become a teacher. For one glorious moment, in 1976, the world was a happy place. I offer the story of Moses by way of introduction because, without knowing it consciously at the time, I learned two lessons from Moses that actually underpin the other 22 lessons. The first lesson, almost a truism, is:

SUCCESS IS REALLY UP TO YOU!

This lesson is best expressed by Maria Robinson:

> *Nobody can go back and start a new beginning, but anyone can start today and make a new ending.*[1]

Moses had almost zero chance of becoming a waiter when I first started teaching him. But he grabbed the opportunity of a willing child eager to help him with both hands. He did not stay a waiter for very long. Moses moved on to bigger and better things, eventually landing an office job and even getting a driver's licence. I remember his pride, years later, when he arrived at the hotel in his company car. Moses taught me that, while how it starts is not up to us, what we make of our life is a result of our own conscious choices and actions.

This brings me to the second lesson, best expressed by a sentence I coined that I now use at the beginning of all my training sessions:

CHANGE IS A VERB!

So many of us are waiting for change, hoping that it will walk through the door one day. It doesn't. In one of my

---

[1] Maria Robinson, *From Birth to One: The Year of Opportunity*, Open University Press, 2003.

favourite cartoons, a man stands in front of an audience and asks: "Who wants change?" Everyone puts up their hands. In the next strip, he asks a different question. No hand goes up. The question he asks is: "Who wants *to* change?"

The bottom line is this: If you want change, you have to start thinking differently and doing things differently. If something is not working for you, the only way for it to be different is to take charge of the change you want to bring about. As you will see in this book, our thoughts are incredibly important, but, ultimately, the universe supports action. Without a conscious effort to *be different* and to *do things differently,* nothing will change.

The lessons contained in this book are offered as handrails to guide you on the process. Let Moses be your inspiration. Against all odds, he succeeded by taking charge of his life. In a twist of fate, how it ended for Moses was not up to him either. He died in 1985, the year I finished school. While visiting his family in KwaZulu-Natal, he was killed in a turf war between the ANC and the IFP. Another sad casualty of apartheid. How Moses chose to spend the years in between was completely a function of his own actions. I trust yours will be too.

* * *

Each lesson contains my general explanation of it, as well as an entry written during the first 22 days of South Africa's Covid-19 lockdown. As with any writing, time and subsequent events change the way we look at things. The lockdown pieces are essentially real-time diary entries, but they also show how the lessons may be applied practically to whatever you are experiencing in your life. The first lockdown was an uncertain time and we forget how little we knew about what life held in store for us. This is true of all life, always. But those three weeks were a pressure cooker of uncertainty and anxiety.

At numerous points throughout my posts, I was at pains to point out that Covid-19 and lockdown had different meanings for each of us. I was acutely aware that many were suffering – both economically and healthwise. My empathy levels had never been higher, and I endeavoured to assist those less fortunate than myself wherever I could. At the same time, I could only live my reality. My lockdown posts, intermingled with the original lessons, were a glimpse into that reality.

Finalising this edition of the book has coincided with a certain 'coming out' of lockdown and a return to 'normality' (whatever that means). During this time of lockdown and beyond, through my work, I have borne witness to a lot of pain and grief. If this book finds you in the midst of suffering, please know that I am not suggesting you can 'think' yourself happy, or that one has to be positive all the time. Suffering, guilt and death (Viktor Frankl's 'tragic triad') are an inevitability while you are alive. As a follower of Frankl, the founder of logotherapy[2], rather than being about merely seeking pleasure, this book is about discovering meaning – not only in the moment, but also in your life as a whole. As Anatole Broyard said, "If 'shrink' is the slang term for

---

2 Logotherapy, a therapeutic approach that helps people find personal meaning in life, was developed by Viktor Frankl after surviving the Nazi concentration camps. His experiences are detailed in his book, *Man's Search for Meaning*, Beacon Press, 1959. Frankl believed that humans are motivated by a "will to meaning", that life can have meaning even in the worst of circumstances, and that the motivation for living comes from finding that meaning (verywellmind.com).

the Freudian analyst, then the logotherapist ought to be called 'stretch'.[3] I trust this book will 'stretch' you towards a life of meaning filled with as many moments of joy as possible.

The first two editions of the book included 'Corona Time' in their title. People found this misleading, believing that the book was about Covid-19, and we have all had enough of the virus! The central message of the book is that present-moment awareness is the key to happiness, growth and success. It felt apt to rename it. Whenever you find this book, I trust that **Twenty-two Lessons for Now** will provide you with food for thought and ways to survive in the AC (After Covid) world in which we all now find ourselves endeavouring to live productive lives of meaning and purpose.

---

3 The New York Times, November 26, 1975. Quoted by Viktor Frankl in *The Unheard Cry for Meaning*, Hodder and Stoughton, 1978.

PROLOGUE: TWO 'PRE-LESSONS'

THE DASH
— LINDA ELLIS

I read of a man who stood to speak at the funeral of a friend. He referred to the dates on the tombstone from the beginning … to the end…
He said what mattered most of all was the dash between those years…
What matters is how we live and love and how we spend our dash…
Are there things you'd like to change? For you never know how much time is left that still can be rearranged.
So when your eulogy is being read, with your life's actions to rehash, would you be proud of the things they say about how you lived your dash?

Copyright © 2020 Inspire Kindness, thedashpoem.com

LESSON 1
TRUST THE PROCESS (TTP)

Life isn't meant to be lived perfectly ...
but merely to be LIVED ... boldly, wildly,
beautifully, uncertainly, imperfectly,
magically LIVED.

— MANDY HALE

Life is so much bigger than we are. At any given moment, things are happening about which we have no clue, and yet, in time, they influence our lives in immeasurable ways. Somewhere, a boy is breaking up with a girl. While she is mourning the break-up, you are somewhere, wondering whether you will ever meet your 'special one'. Some time later, that girl becomes your wife. Life is scheming and planning. It sees her, and it sees you. Life knows what it is doing.

We are so limited by our sensory information – we can only see the small picture. The bigger picture is way beyond our purview. Why then do we worry so much about the things over which we have so little control? Why is it so hard to trust life's process?

I do not believe that worry is innate. I think that human beings have been conditioned to worry. The infant does not worry about its next meal – it simply gets fed. Only when – through abuse or ill-treatment – the food does not come will the infant begin to worry. It is a learned response.

'Be careful of strangers'; 'Don't go into the woods'; 'Watch your back'. These messages condition us to believe that all is not well in the world. Sure, bad things happen, but it is my contention that no amount of worry will prevent the bad things from happening – they will happen, whether we worry about them or not. But so will the good things. The process of life unfolds, regardless of how much anxiety we choose to attach to it. Some even argue that excessive worry and anxiety may actually draw the negative closer, but I don't know whether that is true or not – after all, there is a certain degree of randomness in the world. And then there is cause and effect. Somewhere between '*shit happens*' and '*I am in charge*' lies the human experience.

Given the choice to worry or to trust, I have found that trust serves me better. When you trust the process, you choose to believe that life is unfolding as it should. People will die; you will get sick – it is impossible to be alive without experiencing some degree of suffering. But you will also experience love. And you will also experience good health.

The visual representation of a heartbeat on an Electrocardiography (ECG) machine is a beautiful metaphor for life. Our heartbeat is life itself – a series of ups and downs and highs and lows. And yet, human beings want life to be a straight line. But a straight line is death – it is the complete opposite of what life *is*! Once you understand this, you stop fighting life – you take the good with the bad and the bitter with the sweet.

LESSON 1: TRUST THE PROCESS (TTP)

When Nelson Mandela was inaugurated, he was asked how it felt to be at the top of the mountain. He responded with these memorable words:

> *I have discovered the secret that, after climbing a great hill, one only finds that there are many more hills to climb.*

Somehow, we believe that having achieved a goal, we will receive our much-longed-for straight line. But it doesn't work that way, I'm afraid. There is no respite – not while you are alive! Mandela knew this. At the summit, you can see those other hills. You may certainly rest – the long upward climb may require it, but it will not be long before you have to walk downhill. Soon, the uphill climb will begin again – after all, you're alive! Why would you want a flat line? If you know that life is full of uphills and downhills, why should you worry? Would it not make sense to trust the process instead?

Trust and faith are synonymous. I have met so many people who have faith in God, yet they lack trust. Whatever – or whomever – you choose to call your God, life is God's gift to you. You cannot have faith in God without trusting in life! In my view, you cannot trust the one without trusting the other.

In order to trust life, you must allow it to unfold without feeling the need to *control* it. You must, however, *influence* it every step of the way. Control and influence are not the same thing. Control is the opposite of trust. Influence requires taking proactive steps to create the life you desire, whereas control assumes that all the variables are up to you. They rarely are.

Trust is yours for the taking. Trust the ups and trust the downs. When they stop, so too does life. The troubles don't last, and neither do the gifts – that would be flat-line living, and there is no such thing. When you embrace it all, you will find yourself in harmony with life's rhythm. Half the battle will be won. From this place, you can begin to make your choices.

Welcome to a life of trust. It is the first – and most important – lesson.

> Somewhere between 'shit happens' and 'I am in charge' lies the human experience.

TRUST THE PROCESS – LOCKDOWN DAY 1

When I think about the things that I was 'worried' about in January 2020, here I sit in lockdown – with a whole new set of worries. What a waste of time. That is why I am choosing not to worry right now. I am replacing my worry with trust. Consciously and purposefully.

Do I think about life post-lockdown? Sure. But thoughts and worry are not the same thing. I consciously train my mind not to worry. I breathe deeply when I feel worry and angst take over – then I breathe out the worry and breathe in trust. Deep trust.

This tiny virus is so much bigger than me – than all of

LESSON 1: TRUST THE PROCESS (TTP)

us. We didn't see it coming and we have no control over it. All we can do is our best every day.

So, I continue to trust that this process, this time, will in some way serve a bigger purpose. I don't know what it will be but, as with life, the lessons come after the experience. All I can do is keep myself safe, take the necessary precautions, and trust that how it unfolds is how it is supposed to unfold. If I get Covid-19, I will deal with that. If someone I love gets it, I will deal with that. But I will only deal with it when it happens. I will not let my mind run away from me.

I am my mind. I will train my mind and exercise my ability to reprogramme it – less worry, more trust. I will keep the faith. What my life looks like post-lockdown is as much about what I do *during* lockdown as it is about the forces that are beyond my control.

TTP – Trust The Process.

LESSON 2
MONDAY BEFORE TUESDAY

The one thing we know about the future is that it comes only one day at a time.

— JEFF RICH

It is my experience that one of the greatest reasons we don't achieve our goals is not because we can't, but because we keep taking ourselves out of the present. We plan, we scheme, we dream – and, in the process, we don't actually do anything. Whenever I find myself paralysed by fear or worry, I literally stop and say, "Monday before Tuesday" – this allows me to do what I need to do today. If there is nothing to do today, then so be it – I do nothing. I will do what needs doing tomorrow – tomorrow.

Human beings are not mind readers, but we think that we are. We spend so much time anticipating what someone might do and say that, when we are finally face-to-face with that person, it does not go as we imagined it would. The lesson is the same: deal with reality – deal with what is.

If the past 'was', and the present 'is', what, then, is the future? When I have asked this question at my training sessions, I get all sorts of answers: "What will be", "What could be", "What may be", and so on, but that is not the answer.

The truth is that the future 'is not'. Many people are sceptical when they first hear this. What do you mean, the future is not? Of course there is a future. It is now Monday and tomorrow will be Tuesday. But when it is Tuesday, it will not be the future – it will be the present. The only control I have over Tuesday is what I do on Monday. Ditto for any time in the future. So, protest all you want. Worry all you want about tomorrow and all the future days of your life, but today is the day that needs you to give it your all. [4]

This lesson is nothing new. The 'power of now' has become something of a cliché – popularised by Eckhart Tolle in his book of the same name. [5]

The thing about clichés is that they are usually true. The only thing we can really do with the past is forgive or take revenge. It is unfortunate that English speakers have put the words 'forgive and forget' in the same phrase – as if they are the same thing. But they are not. Because so many people can't forget, they think they can't forgive. Human beings are not forgetters – not of the things that really matter. The big things – the things that require forgiveness – do not require forgetting. You can, however, forgive what is past, recognising that it is the past. At the same time, you can allow the future to be – recognising that it does not exist until it is the present.

And so, we are left with the present. What a delightful word it is in English – a synonym for 'gift'. Today really is a gift. It is life's gift to you. One day, today will be your last day – that's how it works. Don't waste today regretting the past and worrying about the future.

---

[4] I was introduced to this at a workshop called "Breakthrough" that I did in 1988. I do not know who the originator of the exercise was, but s/he is acknowledged with humility and gratitude. This concept changed my life.

[5] Eckhart Tolle, *The Power of Now*, Namaste Publishing, 1997. I highly recommend this book, as well as *A New Earth* by the same author.

LESSON 2: MONDAY BEFORE TUESDAY

Many people think that living in the now means that they must not have dreams or set goals. This is not true. In fact, Viktor Frankl said the following:

> *Man cannot really exist without a fixed point in the future. Under normal conditions, his entire present is shaped around that future point, directed toward it like iron filings toward the pole of a magnet.* [6]

By all means, set goals and dream big, but remember that your goals and dreams require action – and action can only be taken in the present. Do not miss today's rainy day by dreaming of sunshine tomorrow. There is as much joy to be found in today's rain as there is to be found in tomorrow's sun. Today's rain is certain – tomorrow's sunshine is not.

* * *

My father died when I was twenty-three. He was much older than my mother and, growing up, we were reminded of his life insurance policies that would ensure that we – my mother, my sister and I – would be taken care of once he was gone. After he died, my mother, in a desperate attempt to save their ailing business, ceded all his policies to the bank (and other creditors) leaving us with nothing when the business eventually closed. My father spent his entire life being future-focused. There were no overseas trips and there was no lavish spending – he wanted to be certain that his family would be taken care of in the future. But when the future came – surprise, surprise – he was gone, and we were penniless. This does not mean

---

[6] Viktor E Frankl, *The Doctor and the Soul: From Psychotherapy to Logotherapy*, page 104. Souvenir Press, 2004.

that I think one should not save money or take care of the future by investing in policies and annuities. But find the balance between enjoying today and saving for tomorrow.

I wish my father had taken an overseas trip. His life would have been richer for it and, in the final analysis, we would have been no poorer. *Carpe diem*, dear ones, *carpe diem. Seize the day.*

> Do not miss today's rainy day by dreaming of sunshine tomorrow. Today's rain is certain – tomorrow's sunshine is not.

MONDAY BEFORE TUESDAY - LOCKDOWN DAY 2

"How am I going to keep this up?" I ask myself – and I'm on Day 2. Then I remind myself that all I need to do today is write this piece. Tomorrow, I'll write the next one. And the day after, the next one. That is how goals are achieved – you do what needs doing today, and you allow tomorrow to take care of itself. Of course, tomorrow doesn't take care of itself: you do. But take care of tomorrow – tomorrow. First, you need to take care of today – today.

If ever there was a time for present-moment awareness, this is it. We are truly in a situation where all we have is today. Yesterday, in response to my post, I reconnected with someone I last saw in 1999! She asked if we could Skype this morning and we had an amazing 90-minute chat. There was no way I could have anticipated that, yesterday. No amount of thinking (on Saturday) about what I was going to do on Sunday, could have anticipated a beautiful reconnection on Sunday. So, today, I intend to focus only on Sunday. I will take care of Sunday and life will take care of Monday for me.

I am reminded of my favourite piece of dialogue from *Winnie-the-Pooh:*

> *"What day is it?" asked Pooh. "It's today," squeaked Piglet. "My favourite day," said Pooh.* [7]

Today I heard about people who are planning what they intend to do when the lockdown is over. That's more than two weeks away! Don't spend too much time thinking about the 'after'. It's neither guaranteed nor predictable. Sunday before Monday; Monday before Tuesday. Whenever I feel myself going into what 'isn't', I imagine an invisible string between myself and the future and, in my mind, I pull myself back into today. Today, today, today ... be here and stay here. Enjoy the gift of the present. The future is really not ours to tell.

* * *

As fate would have it, the lockdown was extended by two more weeks. Subsequently, we found ourselves in some form of lockdown for more than two years! Life forced us to take it one day at a time. By the time you are reading this, I wonder what your present looks like.

---

[7] A.A. Milne, *Winnie-the-Pooh*, Methuen, 1926.

LESSON 3

THE INFORMATION IS NEUTRAL

Between stimulus and response, there is a space. In that space is our power to choose our response. In our response lies our growth and our freedom.

— VIKTOR E. FRANKL

I walk my dogs every morning but, because I live in Johannesburg, I drive to a park and walk them there. One morning, driving back from the park, I stopped at a stop street – as one does. Cars were coming in both directions, and a pedestrian was waiting to cross. I have a thing for pedestrians – I tend to notice them. To most people in the world, that would sound odd. But South Africans – and Joburg drivers in particular – seem mostly to ignore them. As the traffic flow eased up on both sides of the road, I motioned to the pedestrian to cross. She, unaccustomed to being noticed, hesitated before crossing. As she started walking across the street, the driver of the car behind me hooted. Of course, this all happened in a matter of seconds. And it was early. And it was winter. And – Lord forgive me – as the person hooted, I raised my left hand and showed them a finger. "Bloody rude South African! Can't you see that I'm waiting for the pedestrian to cross?" I muttered under my breath as I pulled a zap sign – becoming that very rude South African in the process. The pedestrian crossed, and I drove the final three hundred metres to my house. As I pulled up to my gate, my phone beeped. It was a text from my friend, Simone. "Nice, Trev," it read. It turns out that Simone had been the person behind me at that stop street – she was taking her children to school, which was in the same area. And she hadn't been hooting at me to drive – she was saying hello! Thankfully, Simone is a good friend and she forgave me for my rudeness.

The hoot was just a hoot – it had no intrinsic meaning. To Simone, the hoot was a "Hello", whereas to me, the hoot was a "Move!" I gave the hoot its meaning, and, having decided what it meant, I reacted. Had I taken one second to breathe, and another to look in my rear-view mirror, I would have interpreted the hoot differently.

Life is full of 'hoots' – bosses, children, spouses, and total strangers are 'hooting' at us all the time. We are bombarded by sensory information everywhere we go. We see, hear, taste, touch, and smell. The sensory information has no absolute meaning – the truth is that the information is neutral. Human beings are meaning-making machines – we are designed that way. But we forget that it is our beliefs that give rise to our reactions to this sensory information, rather than the information itself.

When you understand this, you begin to listen to your self-talk. Being aware of what you say to yourself is the beginning of freedom because as soon as you consciously tune into how you are interpreting what is happening to you, you stop reacting to it. Instead, you begin to respond. A reaction is not a response. We react when we *believe* the sensory information. We respond when we choose our *interpretation* of what is happening to us. It is such a powerful thing to do, and it slows life down in the most beautiful way. We open ourselves up – we are unafraid of what may come our way. We breathe, we consider what is happening, and then, from a place of choice, we decide how we will respond. We begin to become 'response-able'.

> Let life come at you. Don't waste it in reactivity – cherish it in choice.

SOBER is a great breathing space technique, used in recovery circles, to keep reminding yourself that the information is neutral:

S – Stop
O – Observe what's going on (I'm angry, can't think straight, I'm procrastinating)
B – Breathe (Yes, really: take deep, slow breaths)
E – Evaluate the situation (Challenge your thoughts. Could it mean something else?)
R – Respond (Figure out how to proactively contend with the circumstances)

Let life come at you. You have, between your ears, the ability to give meaning to the things that happen to you. What a precious gift! Don't waste it in reactivity – cherish it in choice.

THE INFORMATION IS NEUTRAL – LOCKDOWN DAY 3

We live in the Information Age. We are being bombarded by information in a way that no previous generation has ever experienced. Imagine a daily tweet by Anne Frank about her conditions in the attic. The absurdity of that picture should give you some indication of how we are living and, hence, the absurdity of it all. We cannot afford to be in a reactive mode right now. I understand that there is nothing 'neutral' about the actual Covid-19 virus. It is invisible, and it kills. But we still have, within us, the power of interpretation and, therefore, of response. In the BC (Before Covid) years, I did not have time to complete this project (my book). Now, I do. That is response-ability. I can spend an hour a day watching CNN, freaking out at Trump, or I can spend it in quiet contemplation and writing. I can react to every tweet, newsflash, and horror story. Or I can just be an observer of it – responding only to that which is affecting me personally right now. I am grateful that I have the privilege of choice. My current personal circumstances allow me to give lockdown its meaning.

Yesterday, two beautiful things happened to confirm my beliefs. My friend, Dani, in Israel, shared a metaphysical healer's interpretation of Covid-19. It is life forcing us to go inside. Literally and figuratively. How will I choose to be when I am inside? What will I choose to do when I am inside? Those are the questions I will allow myself to reflect on today.

Another friend, Sam, sent me this text: "I have never felt a greater sense of freedom in my life. It's bizarre. For the first time in my life, I have just surrendered to what

LESSON 3: THE INFORMATION IS NEUTRAL

is because there is *nothing* I can do. I'm facing my biggest fears, and I'm okay. I'm still fighting the fight where I can but, on another level, just being at peace with what is. It's an incredible feeling." That is her interpretation of, and response to, the lockdown.

Neither I nor my friends are in denial. Many people are suffering. My empathy levels have never been higher. At the same time, I can only live my reality. And my reality is as much a function of how I choose to respond, as it is about what is actually 'out there'. Tune out the noise. Go inside. Have a blessed day.

LESSON

DON'T BE ATTACHED TO THE OUTCOME

*Outcomes are for the future –
experiences are for the present.*
— STEFAN BROZIN

Whenever anyone tells me that they are *disappointed*, I ask them, "Who have you appointed?" The question – meant tongue-in-cheek – has some truth in it. Usually, when we are disappointed, it is because someone (or something) has not met the expectations that we have placed on them – or the situation. When we *appoint* someone (or something) and then assume that they (or it) will meet those expectations, we generally end up *dis-appointed*.

The truth is that nobody knows how it is *supposed* to be: things turn out the way they are supposed to turn out – not the way that we have *decided* they need to be. So: take action, make choices, and decide things, but don't attach yourself to the outcomes. Life unfolds just as it should; it is only our expectations that get in the way.

Usually, when we have a choice or a decision to make, we get stuck by playing out the outcome of each choice in our mind's eye. We pretend that we know how things will turn out: if I go this way, this will happen; if I go that way, that will happen. We become so attached to the outcome that we keep ourselves stuck in inaction. The truth is that the only thing life is asking us to do is to make a choice.

Of course, when faced with a choice, you need to do your 'homework' and consider the pros and cons. Evaluate your choices, take action – and then let go of the 'picture' of how it is supposed to be. It rarely turns out the way we think it will. In that way, even after making a decision, you give life permission to unfold in the way that it wants to. Holding on to the outcome to justify the 'rightness' of your choice is a recipe for suffering. All we need to keep doing is making choices, rather than trying to predict the future. [8]

> Bless what you have and, when it is time to let it go, bless the letting go too.

When you take action and allow what follows to take its natural course – no matter how you think it should be – you are practising the Buddhist principle of non-attachment. And while you're busy practising not being attached to the outcome, you might as well go the whole hog – the Buddhists teach that we should be attached to nothing: neither the outcome nor anything else. Buddha is quoted as having said, "The root of all suffering is attachment." Non-attachment is a difficult practice, which

---

[8] This idea is based on Susan Jeffers' "No-Lose Decision-Making Model" as described in her book "Feel the Fear and Do It Anyway", another highly recommended read. Susan Jeffers, *Feel the Fear and Do It Anyway*, Random House, 1987.

LESSON 4: DON'T BE ATTACHED TO THE OUTCOME

can take years to cultivate, but it is worth being mindful of it. The description of non-attachment that I like best is contained on a *Journey* card, written by Brandon Bays and Kevin Billett. [9]

Here is *The Journey* card's musing on non-attachment:

> *Have you been investing importance in the things of life? Have you become attached to items, symbols, tokens, or even people? Practise a light relationship with things, for they are the play dough of reality.*

Don't you love that phrase, '*the play dough of reality*'? Indeed, it is all on loan – you can even love deeply and remain unattached. Life is impermanent, and nothing lasts forever. Whatever you are holding on to today – the outcome, the person, or the things – is all on loan. Live your life in recognition of this fact, and you will live a life of less fear and less pain. Allowing things to unfold the way they are supposed to will also allow for a certain flow – you will experience the freedom that non-attachment brings, allowing life to unfold as it wishes to, without your needing to control its course or its outcome. Bless what you have and, when it is time to let it go, bless the letting go too. It is not easy, but neither is holding on too tightly. Let it come and let it go.

This lesson is particularly helpful for keeping your ego in check. A defining feature of the ego is that it wants it all done 'my way'. Ego wants to control everything – but you cannot control other people or their reactions. Focus on your end of the equation, and leave them to theirs. The same principle applies to our work, especially

---

[9] "The Journey" is a book written by Brandon Bays, who runs workshops of the same name. Brandon's ideas have influenced me tremendously and her cards, two of which I select daily as part of a morning ritual, have played an integral role in my life – as well as those of my clients – who choose a card at the end of their sessions. I will be forever indebted to Kevin Lowe for introducing me to Brandon. Brandon Bays, *The Journey*, Simon & Schuster, 2003.

in the creative fields. All work leaves our hands at some point. If you can accept that you control only the effort that goes in and not the results which come out, you will be mastering your ego. [10]

In 2019, I was blessed to help a beautiful man, Stefan Brozin, write a book about his and his children's experience of losing their wife and mother to cancer. Stefan is living testimony to the lessons I am imparting here. He is one of the finest examples of a human being who comes from as little ego as possible. Stefan's trusting of the process, and his commitment to non-attachment, allowed his wife to die with dignity – and showed me that it is possible to love and be unattached at the same time. [11]

DON'T BE ATTACHED TO THE OUTCOME – LOCKDOWN DAY 4

Several years ago, I worked for a publisher who paid me to stay at home and write. For the two years that I worked for him, he paid me a monthly salary – all of which was offset against future royalties. What this meant was that I would only begin to earn my royalties once he had recouped the money he had 'advanced' me. Needless to say, when my contract with him ended, I owed him a lot of money. I remember thinking that, in the South African book market, he would never be able to sell enough books for me to ever see a royalty cheque. I consciously and deliberately detached from ever being paid royalties. I was grateful for what I had received for those two years, and then I let go of my expectations. I moved on and never gave it a second thought. Fourteen years later – one

---

[10] Adapted: Ryan Holiday, *25 Ways To Kill The Toxic Ego That Will Ruin Your Life*. Medium.com

[11] The book is called *You are here: A story of presence*, by Stefan Brozin, and is available on Amazon and Kindle (published in 2019 by Screenworld Pty Ltd).

LESSON 4: DON'T BE ATTACHED TO THE OUTCOME

week before lockdown – I received an e-mail from the publisher. I read it, and I read it again, and then I wrote him an e-mail to ask if perhaps he had made a mistake. His response was almost immediate: "No, Trevor, the advance is paid back. I told you it would automatically start flowing thereafter."

On the first day of lockdown, I received an amount of money that ensured I wouldn't need to worry about money for the next two months. Can you imagine what that meant to a self-employed person who had just had two contracts put on hold as a result of lockdown? I had no expectations – I detached from this money fourteen years ago. And just when I needed it, it arrived.

Lockdown provides us with ample opportunities to practise non-attachment. Clear out the cupboards, donate the clothes you'll never wear, and give away the books you'll never read. Let go of unrealistic expectations – of yourself and others. Don't let things own you. If your child breaks something, let it go. If your partner doesn't behave the way you think they should, let it go. In fact, let go of your entire "should" list. "Should" is always about expectations. The more "shoulds" you have, the greater will be your disappointment. I will write more about this in **Lesson 9**.

For now, trust that each person is doing their best and that their best and your best are not the same. Concern yourself with yourself, and let others be. Love deeply, but let it be a love free of judgement. Let's all enjoy a deeply loving day, free of expectations or attachment.

LESSON 5

MAKE IT UP AS YOU GO ALONG

*You must be the person you have never had
the courage to be. Gradually, you
will discover that you are that person,
but until you can see this clearly, you
must pretend and invent.*

— PAULO COELHO

Many years ago (when we still met bank managers) I had a meeting with a manager to discuss a loan that I needed. I was so nervous. A million thoughts went through my mind as I waited for him – "Finance is not my thing"; "I won't have the right documentation"; "He'll say no." It turned out that it was his first month in the job, and he was as nervous as I was. I only found this out later in subsequent interactions that I had with him, but, on that day, as I sat opposite him, I did not know.

"What if the client knows more than me?" "What if he asks me a question I can't answer?"

These were the thoughts that were going through his mind. Both of us had put on our 'professional' face and did what most of the world does every day – we were making it up as we went along. As a child, one of my favourite teachers at school was in her first year of teaching, making it up as she went along. I had one of my best and most successful years of teaching with the first class that I taught. In retrospect, and despite my education, I didn't have a clue about what I was doing – I gave it my best shot, and I worked really hard but, for the most part, I was making it up as I went along.

The reason this lesson is so important is that it takes away the fear that others know better than you, that everyone else is an expert, and that 'they' always know what they're doing – they don't! Just like you, they are human beings, which, for the most part, means that they are working out how to do it as they go along.

Yes, there are experts in different fields, so this is not a prescription for arrogance of the 'know it all' type – it's not about knowing it all. It's about trusting yourself enough to know that you are working it out, just like everybody else. When you understand that most of the world is making it up as they go along, you get to stop living in fear. People who trust themselves, trust themselves to work it out.

I worked for a man who sold products and services that did not yet exist. He would listen to the prospective clients' needs and sell them what they needed. He would come to my office, tell me what he had sold, and ask me to work it out or create it. At first, I used to panic and get angry with him, but this man – an entrepreneur of the highest order – got it. He trusted himself – and he trusted me – that we would make it up and present the client with what they needed.

The client was also making it up. They thought they knew what they wanted. We offered or gave them what we thought they needed and, in most cases, both parties worked it out! That's how it works, especially in the world

LESSON 5: MAKE IT UP AS YOU GO ALONG

of work – nobody knows more, and nobody knows better. They know what they know, and you know what you know. Do your best, but don't let the fear of having to know it all get in the way of starting a project, a job, or a business.

> **Don't allow 'not knowing' to get in the way of achieving whatever it is that you wish to achieve.**

This lesson was originally titled 'Pretend', but that confused people – they thought it meant to lie. Making it up as you go along is not about lying – it is about playing the game. My experience has taught me that most people are excellent pretenders – the successful ones, that is. They have learned to cover their fears and insecurities with a veneer of confidence. Confident people are more likely to succeed than those who walk around believing they can't do something because they haven't worked it out yet.

I am not a confident public speaker. I am self-conscious of my voice, but I have been blessed with the gift of being an excellent teacher. Each time I stand up to teach, a little voice whispers in my head, worrying about my voice. But I pretend – I pretend so as not to allow fear to get in the way. For the most part, I succeed – within five minutes of addressing a new group, the fear has vanished, and I am in my zone. Teaching, like public speaking, is a scary thing. You never know what your audience will throw at you, or how they will respond. But that's okay. Whatever happens and whatever question they ask, I make it up as I go along. And if I don't know, I simply tell them, "I don't know."

Don't allow 'not knowing' to get in the way of achieving whatever it is that you wish to achieve. Lower the volume of the voice in your head that is telling you that you don't know enough and maximise the volume of the voice that says, "You'll work it out" – everyone else is!

MAKE IT UP AS YOU GO ALONG – LOCKDOWN DAY 5

I chose this lesson for Day 5 as I sat down with some apprehension today. "Am I going to be able to keep this up?" "What if it gets boring?" "What if the message doesn't land?" "What message is right for today?" All these thoughts are the thoughts of needing to know. Today's lesson reminds me that it's okay to make it up as I go along, that I don't need to be an expert, and that not every lesson has to be profound or mind-blowing. I'm making this up as I go along and, guess what, it's all right. Nobody knows better than me. Every single one of us is making it up as we go along, here. None of us has lived through a pandemic or lockdown. Anyone who tells you that there is a 'right' way to do this thing is kidding themselves. Trust yourself. Do it your way. If you get it 'wrong', it's okay. Other lessons are coming up to help with that. For today, I will trust myself enough to know that, like everyone else, I'm working it out as I go.

LESSON 5: MAKE IT UP AS YOU GO ALONG

"Fake it 'til you make it" is the better-known version of this lesson. Like 'Pretend', I don't like either of these versions because they both imply a level of deception. That is not the lesson's intention. Rather, this lesson serves to remind us that we don't have to wait for everything to be in place, or for lockdown to be over, before starting. It is the antidote to procrastination. Just start! The universe supports action and, if you do the work, it will come to your aid. And, should you get it wrong, or circumstances change, you can course-correct.

Today I will trust myself to work it out. Tomorrow, I'll work it out some more. Let's trust ourselves today – not to be experts, not to get it right, just to make it up one day at a time. Happy making-it-up day!

LESSON 6
BE GRATEFUL

Piglet noticed that even though he had a Very Small Heart, it could hold a rather large amount of Gratitude.

— A.A. MILNE *(Winnie-the-Pooh)*

I start every day with two prayers. The first prayer – *Modeh Ani* – is from my Jewish faith. It means "Grateful am I: I offer thanks to You, living and eternal King, for You have mercifully restored my soul within me; Your faithfulness is great."

After I have said my Jewish prayer, I say a traditional African prayer. I learned it from a Sangoma – an African traditional healer – whom I visited some years ago for a few sessions of healing. The prayer begins with the words "Thokoza, amadlozi". These words are literally an expression of gratitude for my ancestors, who include my father, my grandparents, and my nanny, Monica – whom I see as one of my 'guiding spirits' – who brought me up and taught me to respect all people.

One of my favourite quotes is by French philosopher Pierre Teilhard de Chardin:

> *We are not human beings having a spiritual experience. We are spiritual beings having a human experience.*[12]

---

[12] This is attributed to Pierre Teilhard de Chardin in *The Joy of Kindness* (1993), by Robert J. Furey, p. 138.

By creating my own ritual and combining two prayers from my heritage – one from my religious heritage (Jewish) and the other from what I consider to be my ethnic heritage (African) – I have found a language of my own with which to address my Supreme Being. While I am not a conventionally religious person, I am certainly a person filled with faith. I am convinced that there is a power greater than myself that pervades the Universe, and that is (somehow) looking over the human race as we make our way through life. I do not believe that this greater power is a punishing being – or even a rewarding being, for that matter. Instead, I believe there is a plan for each of us and that, depending on the choices and actions we take, the plan has the potential to work out well or not to work out well. The way it works out, however, is still part of a master plan which we, as human beings, are not fully able to comprehend. I live with a deep and abiding sense of being 'looked after'. Gratitude for the human experience you are having will carry you in ways you cannot even begin to imagine.

After many years of praying in this way, I discovered Frankl's definition of religion:

> *God is the partner of your most intimate soliloquies… Whenever you are talking to yourself in utmost sincerity and ultimate solitude – he to whom you are addressing yourself may justifiably be called God.* [13]

Whether I am talking to myself or to God, what is significant about my two prayers is that they both start with the same word – Thanks. And that is, ultimately, what this lesson is about. By uttering these two prayers, both of

---

[13] Viktor E. Frankl, *The Unheard Cry for Meaning: Psychotherapy and Humanism*, Simon and Schuster, 2011.

which are about gratitude, I acknowledge deep within my soul that, despite whatever life is presenting me with at the moment, I am able to handle it from a place of trust and a place of faith – knowing that both my Creator and my Ancestors are guarding and guiding me. For that, I am eternally grateful. I am grateful even when – on the surface – it appears that things are not going my way. Who am I to question the master plan? How am I to know that these present circumstances will not serve me in some way? Like **Lesson 1 (Trust The Process)**, this lesson encourages us to embrace life as it is, rather than as we think it 'should' be.

> Gratitude for the human experience you are having will carry you in ways you cannot even begin to imagine.

Gratitude is, of course, not reserved only for prayer. From a scientific point of view, our brains have a built-in negativity bias that makes us more likely to remember bad experiences than good ones. This happens because negative events trigger an adrenaline rush that engraves negative feelings and memories in the brain. A consistent gratitude practice can literally re-wire your brain to overcome this bias.[14] A popular, slightly cutesy, meme has it that 'gratitude = great attitude'. But there is truth

---

[14] Source: For this, and other scientific benefits of gratitude, see: www.happiness.com

in this. Gratitude is a state of mind. From Ancient Rome where the philosopher, Cicero, called gratitude "the 'mother' of all human feelings" to 21st century motivational speaker Zig Ziglar, who described gratitude as "the healthiest of all human emotions", an attitude of gratitude pervades people who have an optimistic and hopeful outlook.

Human beings are interesting creatures – when we find ourselves at the bottom of life's pulse, as described in **Lesson 1 (TTP)**, we look skywards and lament, "Why me?" When we find ourselves at the top, we look skywards and say, "Thank you". Enlightened souls do the opposite. When they are in trouble, they say, "Thank you" – for the trouble shall pass, and in time they will understand the gifts that it brought. When fortune smiles on them, they say, "Why me?" – humbly acknowledging the gift that has come to them. This practice is so counter-intuitive that it almost sounds absurd, but you should try it next time you find yourself at a high or low point.

Albert Einstein said that the most important question facing humanity is: "Is the universe a friendly place?" If you believe, as I do, that it is a friendly – but not always easy – place, then we need to stay grateful always. Einstein ends his treatise with the following memorable words: "God does not play dice with the universe." Gratitude is its own reward. The more you are grateful, the more there is to be grateful for. Where you focus is where you will go and what you focus on expands. When a loved one who has been suffering dies, we are often faced with conflicting emotions of grief and relief. Finding a way to reconcile these emotions is, for me, akin to finding a way to stay grateful even when we are hurting. It's difficult, but we have already accepted that flat-line living is not what we are after!

Robert Emmons, who has dedicated his life to studying the science of gratitude, says:

> *... It is precisely under crisis conditions when we have the most to gain by a grateful perspective on life. In the face of demoralization, gratitude has the power to energize. In the face of brokenness, gratitude has the power to heal. In the face of despair, gratitude has the power to bring hope. In other words, gratitude can help us cope with hard times.*

Emmons makes the vital distinction between feeling grateful and being grateful. You do not have to ignore or deny your pain or suffering in order to be grateful. Even in tough times, you can find something to be grateful for, albeit momentarily; happy memories, supportive people and acts of kindness. Emmons continues:

> *Processing a life experience through a grateful lens does not mean denying negativity. It is not a form of superficial 'happiology'. Instead, it means realising the power you have to transform an obstacle into an opportunity. It means reframing a loss into a potential gain, recasting negativity into positive channels for gratitude.*[15]

Much like the next lesson (**Lesson 7: Practise Patience**), gratitude requires practice and discipline. That is why I encourage all my clients to incorporate a daily gratitude ritual and/or gratitude journal into their lives. Never miss an opportunity to say, "Thank you". Whether it be an e-mail or a text, if someone does something that is worthy of appreciation, express your gratitude. Gratitude – received or offered – makes us feel better and enhances our mood.

---

[15] www.greatergood.berkeley.edu

Gratitude also makes you more resilient. No matter how hard life may be, gratitude shifts your focus, and your energy, from what you don't have to what you do have, and from what is not working to what is working. That is the power of gratitude – and there is so much to be grateful for!

BE GRATEFUL – LOCKDOWN DAY 6

Based on feedback from yesterday's post, I suspect that some of us had a hard day. That's okay. It's hard to stay 'positive'. I think it's totally okay not to be positive all the time. Walking past a block of flats yesterday, I heard what sounded like a family having a fight. In that moment I was grateful for the fact that I don't have children in need of entertainment (or food) at this time. But it also gave me a glimpse into the reality of this lockdown. This is not an easy thing to endure. At the same time, I thought to myself, "I hope this family is having moments of gratitude for each other, for the fact that they have each other, a flat to stay in, a supermarket round the corner, sunshine to walk in, garbage men to collect their rubbish, internet to connect to the world, TV to watch, neighbours to call on, lungs that are not infected by Covid-19, medical aid should they need …" The list goes on. In 2019 BC, we took a lot of things for granted. As a wonderful meme that did the rounds during lockdown, said:

Now that I've cleared your schedule, let's talk.
— GOD

My friend Trish, with whom I was chatting on Tuesday, expressed the following sentiment: "Every morning, when

LESSON 6: BE GRATEFUL

I get in the shower, I am grateful for the hot water. When I go into my garden, I notice the birds. I stand on the grass, I am grateful for my garden, for my space, for my food, for my husband, and my health." Trish has suffered from numerous serious health issues. Suddenly she sees herself as healthy. She is grateful to be alive, uninfected, and not in need of medical care.

> In my experience, gratitude and generosity are roommates.

Lockdown – for those of us privileged enough to be well, to have space and time, family to be with, friends who check in, money for food, social media to connect us to the world, a door to close when the noise gets too much – is gratitude time. It is also a time for us to help, wherever possible, those who are less fortunate than us. Gratitude shifts my focus and my energy. It also makes me a more generous person. In addition to a gratitude ritual, I also encourage my clients to incorporate a random act of kindness into their daily lives.

I make a list every morning of five things for which I am grateful. Some days it's a stretch, but I force myself to get there. Today I'm grateful for garbage men, coffee, rainy weather, love, and breath.

What are you grateful for, today?

LESSON 7
PRACTISE PATIENCE

*Have patience with all things,
but first of all with yourself.*
— SAINT FRANCIS DE SALES

When my niece Keshie (for whom this book was originally written) was small, she was so impatient. She always wanted everything – now! She hated waiting for food to be ready, for the drive to a place or, heaven forbid, to be told that I couldn't read to her – now! I taught her the silly children's rhyme, "Patience is a virtue; Virtue is a grace; Grace is a little girl who wouldn't wash her face." I have no idea what the rhyme means but patience truly is a virtue. It is a quality worth taking the time to develop.

There is a Native American practice known as 'animal medicine', in which it is believed that each animal represents a different type of 'medicine' – or healing. When we become aware of what a certain animal represents, we can take the steps to create changes in our life. The animal that resonates most for me is the ant. Ant medicine is about patience. Have you ever watched ants building a nest? Each tiny ant carries one small twig at a time. Back and forth they go – back and forth. There is no greater lesson in patience than to watch an ant carry a twig. Of course, one ant cannot do the job alone, so not only is ant medicine about patience, but it is also about the tribe and working together – in patience. Ant medicine is about cooperating with your tribe in harmony and wisdom towards a common goal, knowing that your patience will be rewarded. We can't speed up time and no amount of fretting will make it happen faster. Patiently do what needs doing; the big picture will emerge in time.

A few years ago, I started working for myself, after nine years of being employed. I left the safety and security of a monthly salary to throw myself into the big, wide world of self-employment. I knew, going into this new venture, that I would need to call on ant medicine to guide my way. I wrote a little mantra on a card, which I placed next to my laptop so that I could see it every day. It said: "My time frame is not the Universe's time plan".

I realised early on that setting myself up as an 'entrepreneur' would require me to exercise patience. I knew that building a business was going to take time and that any attempt to force life to make it happen quicker, was going to cause me pain and distress. People don't get back to me when I think they should; the deal doesn't land the way I thought it would; things aren't moving quickly enough – round and round, this mind talk can be so exhausting! But then I remember ant medicine and the virtue of patience. I breathe, and I remember what it takes to build a nest – one twig at a time.

It is the same as writing a book, or any achievement for that matter. One word, one sentence, one paragraph, one chapter – the creative process, like life itself, cannot be hurried along. If everything is happening exactly as it is

LESSON 7: PRACTISE PATIENCE

supposed to be, and Divine right timing is always in play, then who are we to want to speed up time – what a waste of energy! A part of me wishes I had known this when I was younger. As a child, all I wanted was for time to pass – as quickly as possible! As an adult, I look back with such nostalgia on certain parts of my childhood and wish that I hadn't been in such a hurry for them to pass.

> **My time frame is not the Universe's time plan.**

We need not only to be patient with ourselves – but also to be patient with others. Not everyone needs to see the world in the same way that we do. I was a teacher for many years, and I believe that one of the gifts – with which I am blessed – is a tremendous amount of patience. Patience is a skill that can be learned and nurtured. The world is full of people who may not know what you know. Exercise patience with them. There will be times when others know more than you. If they are not patient with you, stop and request that they be patient with you. Recognise that we all have different strengths and skills. Work patiently in those areas to achieve your goals. And allow others to do the same.

Practising patience requires that we learn to tolerate

others. "I am not you; you are not me" is a useful tool in this regard. In practice, this means remembering that we are all different. We know different things; we do things differently and at different speeds. But together we are stronger. If we add patience to the mix, we become kinder and more tolerant of each other.

> I am not you;
> you are not me.

Many people are aware of the "marshmallow experiment" which was used to demonstrate that the children who were able to delay gratification had a greater likelihood of success later in life. The original experiment has since been criticised for not taking into account socio-economic differences (i.e. it is easier to delay gratification when you are used to getting/having things). Be that as it may, an "I want it now" attitude usually just ends in disappointment and dramas. If you struggle with patience, make yourself wait for things. You will become more patient as you find ways to delay gratification.

Ant medicine teaches us patient collaboration, and collaboration requires respect, empathy, tolerance and trust. Patience will assist you to focus on the best opportunities, rather than jumping at everything that comes your way. It also makes it easier to say 'no' and helps you to avoid making decisions in a rush. As long as you are putting in the work, and course-correcting where necessary, practise patience. Your patience will be rewarded in time.

Of course, the best tool for mastering this lesson is **Lesson 2 (Monday Before Tuesday)**. It is hard to be patient if you are not mindful (i.e. in the present). Usually, we are impatient because something is not happening when we think it should be happening. No amount of fretting, or dramatic behaviour, will speed up its arrival. And, on a metaphysical level, the time is always right. So, breathe, find a way to see the gift in the timing, and keep practising patience.

PRACTISE PATIENCE – LOCKDOWN DAY 7

I chose today's lesson after my sister phoned me yesterday to say, "How am I going to do this for another two weeks?" My heart lurched. I'm really taking this one day at a time, but suddenly, the thought of another two weeks made me feel slightly queasy. There is one day at a time and then there are another fourteen days (or more).

And then I remembered ant medicine.

We need ant medicine now more than ever before. We are playing a long game here. The search for a vaccine, the adjustment to a new way of being and doing, hours spent at home, bored children, frustrated partners, dwindling cash reserves … they all require us to practise patience. We can't hurry this thing up and life is forcing us to learn patience. If you are not a naturally patient person, best you start exercising the patience muscle. Failure to do so risks opening yourself up to greater frustration, resentment and anger.

> Be patient with others.
> Not everyone needs to see the world
> in the same way that we do.

While this lesson is not about tribal togetherness, the other side of ant medicine is that ants work together to create their nest. There is no question that Covid-19 is unifying us in ways we could not have imagined previously. By holding up a mirror to our lives, the pandemic is reminding us of how much we need each other. We need to be patient with ourselves, but we also need to be patient with our fellow human beings – our tribe.

As we enter Week Two, let's make a determined effort to be patient with ourselves and others. This beautiful piece comes from a book called *Time for Joy* by Ruth Fishel. It seems apt for today's lesson:

> *There are days when I might have to sit back and wait. I might have to wait for the right time ... the right energy ... the right answer ... I cannot always have the energy that I want or the answers or the*

LESSON 7: PRACTISE PATIENCE

time or the right person in my life. These days are difficult. These are the times to pause and rest. There are days when other people's energies are involved with my answers and they will fall into place in the right time and I will know what to do. Today I wait in peace ... [16]

---

[16] Joy Fishel: *Time for Joy: Daily Affirmations*, Simon and Schuster, 1998.

LESSON 8
GIVE IT A NAME

People will forget what you said, people will forget what you did, but people will never forget how you made them feel.

— MAYA ANGELOU

Brandon Bays, in the 'Emotions' Journey Card, says that "to feel is a defining human experience, so welcome your emotions … they are the gateway to the soul." A lot of this book is about "head stuff". Some say that thoughts precede feelings; others that feelings come first. I happen to believe that our feelings arise from our thoughts, but I also know that I often just have a "feeling" about something, so I am not sure that is very important where our feelings actually come from. What is important, however, is that we feel our feelings (not think them!). Think your thoughts and feel your feelings. Name them, embody them, express them, and use them to guide you.

We have become accustomed to responding to "How are you?" with "I'm good", or "I am fine" – phrases that have become standard ways to describe how we are feeling, whether we're feeling that way or not. The problem is that 'good' and 'fine' are not feelings. On the continuum of feeling words from sad to happy, and angry to scared, 'good' and 'fine' do not feature – they are simply cop-outs. Similarly, we also say that we feel 'bad', but 'bad' is not a feeling either. When you are feeling bad, you are feeling something else – guilt, remorse, sadness, even anger. Like 'good', 'bad' is a cop-out that allows us either not to identify what we are truly feeling, or simply to choose not to share what we are really feeling.

If we are growing as human beings, it is essential that we know how to give names to our feelings. Susan David, whom I am proud to say I knew when she was at Wits,[17] has become a leading expert on the topic of feelings. In her book *Emotional Agility*, which I highly recommend, Dr David says:

> *Emotional agility means being aware and accepting of all your emotions, even learning from the most difficult ones. It also means getting beyond conditioned or pre-programmed cognitive and emotional responses (your hooks) to live in the moment with a clear reading of present circumstances, respond appropriately, and then act in alignment with your deepest values.*[18]

Don't run from difficult emotions, You don't have to be 'happy' all the time. But the best way out is through; name your feelings, feel them fully, and use them to guide you.

We have forgotten not only how to express what we are feeling but we don't allow ourselves to really feel our feelings. "Claim it, aim it, dump it!" is a useful technique in this regard. First you have to *own* the feeling. This is best done by giving it a name. Thereafter, you need to *do*

---

[17] The University of the Witwatersrand, Johannesburg, South Africa.

[18] Susan David, *Emotional Agility: Get Unstuck, Embrace Change, and Thrive in Work and Life*, Avery, NY, 2016.

something with the feeling – this is what is meant by "aim it". If you are angry with someone, tell them. Similarly, if you love someone, tell them. Having claimed it and aimed it, you then have the choice to "dump it" – or not. "Dump it", of course, is more relevant to the negative feelings, but you cannot dump the feeling until you have identified it and done something with it. [19]

The word 'emotion' comes from the Latin word *emovere*, which means 'to move out or remove'. Feelings must be expressed – they must 'come out'. If they don't – in the case of negative feelings – they will simply be displaced or, even worse, become stored. Stored negative emotions cause dis-ease – they literally have the ability to make you sick.

> If we are growing as human beings, it is essential that we know how to give names to our feelings.

GIVE IT A NAME – LOCKDOWN DAY 8

We all need to keep ourselves as healthy as possible right now. Don't ignore the role that your feelings play in this regard. Now is the time to feel our feelings and to name them. I can't remember a time when I have had more

---

[19] I learned this tool at a workshop called "The Turning Point", which I attended in Melbourne in the '90s. I do not know its original source but acknowledge it with gratitude.

feelings in the space of a day than this past week. I go from optimistic and excited to pessimistic and fearful – and then back again. I check in with myself often. I ask myself how I am feeling, find the right word, and then I take action from that place. I switch off the news, put on music; phone a friend, have a moan and go back to feeling happy. As with my thoughts, I let my feelings come and go. I don't dwell there for too long. This too shall pass; this too shall pass.

> Think your thoughts and feel your feelings. Name them, embody them, express them, and use them to guide you.

As fate would have it, I watched an interview with the philosopher, Alain de Botton, on BBC this morning. I found the interview online so that I could record what he said. I certainly could not have said it better:

> *What helps connection is the capacity to admit one's vulnerability … that one might be at risk of feeling lonely. If there's a silver lining in the terrible situation we find ourselves in, it is that it's perhaps easier than it's ever been to say you're afraid, you're feeling isolated. All those things that we have such a hard time admitting to are now much easier to admit to*

LESSON 8: GIVE IT A NAME

> *... The way to make a friend is to reveal that you're scared, that you're broken inside, that you're maybe confused ... All of this is normally so hard to admit because we're supposed to be having a terrific life. The one thing that this crisis has spared us is the pressure to be content. It has allowed us to reveal the emergency that is being alive ... we're always at risk of anxiety, of panic, of loneliness ... we are now more than ever able to share in the vulnerability that was always there ... even though we can't have presence, we can have connection ... and in a way it's always better to have connection than presence ...* [20]

Today I will be connecting with my good friend, Lauren, who lives in London with whom I have not spoken for a long time. I am so excited to speak to her.

Connect with someone today from an honest feeling place. Happy Feeling Day!

---

20 twitter.com/bbcnewsnight/status/1246724279783305217 (still available as at May 2022).

LESSON 9
WATCH THOSE EXPECTATIONS

I'm not in this world to live up to your expectations and you're not in this world to live up to mine.

— BRUCE LEE

This is a tough one. When we are little, we are read fairy tales that tell us that the Prince and Princess "lived happily ever after". There are no sequels in fairy tales. We grow up believing in "happily ever afters". When we are a little older, adults ask us what we want to be 'when we're big'. We dream and we fantasise. We believe that we will meet the perfect mate, find the perfect career, and be happy ever after.

All we are really being taught is to have expectations and, put bluntly, expectations mess us up. You see, expectations are rarely about reality – they are about making demands on reality. When reality does not accord with our demands of how it should be, we end up disappointed. Unfulfilled expectations are a breeding ground for resentment. Keep your expectations realistic and focused on yourself. You cannot control others. When we watch those expectations, we set ourselves up for a life free of blame and resentment.

There is, of course, a strong correlation between

this lesson and **Lesson 4 (Don't be Attached to the Outcome)**, but this lesson is subtler – it commands that you eliminate three words from your vocabulary: 'should', 'could' and 'would', or, as I like to call them 'shoulda, coulda, woulda'. Guess what? He 'should' have, you 'could' have, if only they 'would' – but he *didn't*, you *aren't*, and they *won't*!! It's as simple as that. Life does not have to be fair; everyone does not need to like you; and you cannot expect to change others. Our expectations get in the way of dealing with what *is*. Life is not there to meet your expectations – in fact, the opposite is true. Life is calling you to meet its demands. Are you listening?

> Life is not there to meet your expectations; life is calling you to meet its demands.

A few years ago, I became aware of the importance of intentions, and, for a while, was confused about whether intentions were expectations. They are not. Now, while I set intentions all the time, I continue to watch my expectations. What follows is the best explanation of the difference between intentions and expectations that I have been able to find:

LESSON 9: WATCH THOSE EXPECTATIONS

> *Intention comes to modern English from Latin 'intendere'; meaning, 'to give consideration, turn to or focus one's attention, to have a plan, to think, conjecture or propose' ... an intention is simply an impulse, which gives structure and direction to creative energy. Expectation is a hope that something will happen. It comes from an ego state that is identified or attached to the outcome.* [21]

When we commit to an intention, we put in place a process to achieve something that we want. When we attach to an expectation, we simultaneously attach to an outcome and begin to make demands of life – that things need to happen in the way we think they should. It is not for us to have expectations of life – rather, life has expectations of us. That is the underlying tenet of logotherapy, the therapy to which I subscribe, and which has fundamentally changed my life. Logotherapy is the brainchild of Viktor Frankl, a Holocaust survivor, who found his life's calling in a concentration camp. Filled with expectations of how his life would be, this young doctor instead found himself in Auschwitz with his entire family gone, facing the horrors of a life of starvation and filth. He was exposed to the worst of humanity, and yet he found a way of rising above his circumstances. He did this in many ways, but there is no doubt that one of the major ways in which he did this was by asking himself the question, "What is life calling me to do?" In the depths of his hell on Earth, Frankl was able to let go of how he believed it should be.

---

[21] www.coachcampus.com

Rather, he looked inwards and discovered that:

> ... *it did not really matter what we expected from life, but rather what life expected from us.* [22]

When we focus on what we want life to give us, we become victims. When we focus on what life wants from us, we become victors (pardon the pun).

What Viktor Frankl learned, and subsequently taught, is that we have been given our lives for a purpose:

> *We are called by Life to give meaning to our individual lives. As we respond to the call, make the right choices, do the right thing, we give shape to our lives. Our destinies become manifest. We draw nearer to the goal, to the realisation of the very meaning of our lives. Our stories take shape. Our lives become unique, irreplaceable. We make our mark.* [23]

Expectations get in the way; they create a picture of life before it even happens. This does not mean that you cannot have hopes and dreams – of course, you must. But hopes and dreams are not the same as expectations. There is a 'demand' associated with expectations that I believe gets in the way of life unfolding the way it wants to – you will never know how it is going to be. Take a simple example of the party that you have been waiting to go to, for weeks. You get there, and it's nothing like you expected it to be. You are disappointed. The opposite is also true – the party that you didn't want to go to, turns out to be the best night you've had in years.

---

22 Viktor E Frankl, *Man's Search for Meaning*, page 77. Beacon Press, 1959.

23 Viktor E Frankl, *Man's Search for Meaning*, page 77. Beacon Press, 1959.

LESSON 9: WATCH THOSE EXPECTATIONS

Why does that happen? With the latter, you had few or no expectations, and life surprised you. Life is like that – it is full of surprises. So, by all means, set intentions, hope, and dream, but when the moment arrives, let events unfold without your fantasies getting in the way. Reality may prove to be better than the picture you have in your head of how it 'ought' to be.

> **Reality may prove to be better than the picture you have in your head of how it 'ought' to be.**

WATCH THOSE EXPECTATIONS – LOCKDOWN DAY 9

2019 was an extremely hard year for me, but 2020 was going to be '20-plenty'. It has two '2s" in it, and 2 is my number. This was going to be my year. How many of us expressed the sentiment on New Year's Eve that "2020 can only be better than 2019"? We had so many expectations of this year – we knew that it was going to be "the best year ever".

As the Afrikaans saying goes, "Kyk hoe lyk ons nou!" ["Look at us now!"].

If ever there was a time to watch those expectations and replace them with intentions, lockdown is it. My intentions have become a daily exercise. I have almost no expectations – of myself or others. And certainly not of life. All I know is that life is asking me to stay inside, to write, to work from home, to eat, to sleep and to breathe. And to stay healthy. And so, each day, I do my best to live up to life's demands of me. Ironically, in 2019 BC, life seemed to be making so many demands of me.

> When we watch those expectations, we set ourselves up for a life free of blame and resentment.

Now its demands are actually quite simple. Why would I let my expectations get in the way? I have completely let go of my picture of how I think it should be, what I think the government should or should not be doing, and how other people should be behaving. I am not counting down to the end of lockdown – that would be an expectation. The less I expect, the more I seem to get.

It is easier to set intentions in normal life, of course. But even now, during lockdown, I'm watching my intentions. I prefer to go with intentions that keep it simple, in the now, and only about things I can influence.

The rest of the time it is just about listening to life and following its course.

For today, let's watch those expectations of ourselves, of others, and of life. Let's set intentions that are manageable and do what life is expecting of us, rather than demanding anything of it. Happy Intention Day.

LESSON 10
BE REAL

This above all – to thine own self be true.
— **WILLIAM SHAKESPEARE** (Polonius, in *Hamlet*)

This lesson is inspired by one of my favourite pieces of writing. It comes from a children's book called *The Velveteen Rabbit*, by Margery Williams.

> "Real isn't how you are made," said the Skin Horse. "It's a thing that happens to you. When a child loves you for a long, long time, not just to play with, but REALLY loves you, then you become Real."
> "Does it hurt?" asked the Rabbit.
> "Sometimes," said the Skin Horse, for he was always truthful. "When you are Real you don't mind being hurt."
> "Does it happen all at once, like being wound up," he asked, "Or bit by bit?"
> "It doesn't happen all at once," said the Skin Horse, "You become. It takes a long time. That's why it doesn't happen often to people who break easily, or have sharp edges, or who have to be carefully kept. Generally, by the time you are Real, most of your hair has been loved off, and your eyes drop out and you get loose in the joints and very shabby. But these things

> *don't matter at all, because once you are Real you can't be ugly, except to people who don't understand."* [24]

I don't think I was *real* when I was growing up – I was too scared to be real. I was afraid of the bullies, the popular people and the adults who wanted me to be what I wasn't. I think it takes a lot of bravery to be real when you are small. Some people manage to be real – perhaps they have a confidence that I did not have. It took me a long time to be able to say to the world, in the words of what has become a gay anthem – *I am what I am*. I wish I had known a lot earlier that 'real' was an option. I think I would have saved myself a great deal of pain.

But what exactly does it mean to be real? And, also, does this not contradict **Lesson 5 (Make it Up as You Go Along)**? Let me begin with a philosophical answer. These rules are not scientific – sometimes the lessons may seem to contradict each other. Life is not about black and white – life happens in the grey. You often need to work it out for yourself – sometimes, you need to fake it and sometimes you need to be real! The key is not to fake it when real is called for, and not to go for real when a little bit of pretending is called for.

If that sounds confusing, welcome to life – I really wish I had a more profound answer. Faking it till I made it has served me in specific situations but being real – as a general rule for life – has served me more. You see, I think that people are naturally attracted to real. I believe that so many people are busy pretending to be what they are not, that when you present your real self, they are not only surprised, but they are also naturally (and magnetically) drawn to you.

---

[24] Margery Williams, *The Velveteen Rabbit*, pages 4-5. New York: Square Fish, 2008.

LESSON 10: BE REAL

It's really difficult to be what you are not – it takes energy – and hiding away eventually begins to catch up with you (and cost you) as you grow older. You don't have to wait to become real, like the Skin Horse. You can start early. You are already who you are – allow the world to see you in all your glory. I heard a wonderful little expression once. I have Simone (my zap sign friend) to thank for this one too! (Thanks, Sim.) It goes like this:

Some will; some won't.
Some do; some don't.
So what?
Who's next?

What this means is that some people will 'get' you, and some won't. Some will love you, and some won't. So what? I needed to be liked so badly for so long that I sometimes still forget that it really doesn't matter if not everybody likes me. Isn't that a strange thing about the human condition? We don't like everybody, yet we need everybody to like us. It's such nonsense. If someone doesn't like you for who you are, move on. There is a caveat to this, and probably to all the lessons. It is the universal law of "Do no harm". The reason I am sharing this with you here is that people sometimes feel that they can be honest without limitations or boundaries – I don't believe that this is true. You cannot excuse bad behaviour with an egotistical "This is Me". If your actions or words are causing harm to yourself or others, then you're applying being real in the wrong context. Being mean is not the same as being real.

The effectiveness of your being real will show up most in your relationships. If they are generally happy and fulfilling, then 'real' is working for you. If your relationships are marked by conflicts and drama, you may have to rethink how your 'real' is coming across. Always look to the results of your life to gauge what is working and what may need work.

> Find people with whom you can be real. It is one of the ingredients for a happy life.

As you journey through this world – hopefully doing as much good as you can – find people who love and accept you for who you are *in your truth*. One of my favourite lines in poetry comes from Emily Dickinson:

The soul selects her own society [25]

Isn't that lovely? Your soul – the essence of who you really are – will find its people. Find people with whom you can be real. It is one of the ingredients for a happy life.

BE REAL – LOCKDOWN DAY 10

It strikes me as a little ironic that our current 'hiding away' is revealing ourselves to ourselves – and to each other. Stripped of all activities and distractions, we are meeting ourselves. The pandemic is really a mirror – not just on a personal level, but also on a societal level. Now, we can't

---

[25] "The Soul selects her own Society" (303) by Emily Dickinson, 1862.

LESSON 10: BE REAL

ignore the poor or the homeless or the shack dwellers. Similarly, we can't ignore our relationships, our fears, or our anxieties. It is impossible to spend so much time with yourself or your loved ones without some cracks starting to appear.

Leonard Cohen wrote:

> *Ring the bells that still can ring.*
> *Forget your perfect offering.*
> *There is a crack in everything,*
> *that's where the light gets in.* [26]

How beautiful is that? Interestingly, the lyrics come from his song called "Anthem" off the 1992 album called … wait for it … "The Future" (I rest my case). Being real is about not needing to be perfect. It's about letting the light in through the cracks. It's about seeing our messy selves and letting others see us too. We, like the natural world, are being given an opportunity to heal. Whether the world will actually change is beyond my control. But my own change is up to me.

I have some interesting truths to confront as I face another two weeks of lockdown. I suspect we all do. My intention is to keep it as real as possible, to own the cracks, and to let the light in. Happy real day!

---

[26] Leonard Cohen, "Anthem" on the album *The Future*, 1992.

LESSON 11
TELL THE TRUTH FASTER (TTTF)

*If we are not ashamed to think it,
we should not be ashamed to say it.*
— MARCUS TULLIUS CICERO

TELL THE TRUTH FASTER – LOCKDOWN DAY 11 (PART 1)

Today I'm switching my post around and starting with my lockdown post, as I reflect on this process to which I committed eleven days ago. Many of you have responded very positively, both in public comments and private messages, and the lessons seem to be resonating. I am incredibly grateful to all of you for your feedback and love.

Today's lesson is what I like to call TTP's cousin – Tell The Truth Faster (TTTF). So, in that spirit, for people who are journeying with me through these posts, I thought I'd share some truths. That feels more authentic than the original chapter (some of which I have obviously shared below, with some editing to suit 2022). I have struggled with commitment all my life; I will leave the reasons to my therapist to dissect. This lockdown feels more like a commitment than a prison sentence. I can't get out of this one. It frees me up somewhat when I see it as a commitment – to myself and for the greater good of all of us. It is irresponsible not to commit to self-isolation.

I feel the same way about these posts. I promised, and

now I can't back out. It's getting harder (there's me Telling The Truth Faster). When I started writing this book, I did not intend it to be for public consumption. It was a private gift of love for my niece, and my nephews too – but Covid-19 arrived before either of their 18th birthdays when I intended to gift them with the Lessons. Some of the chapters are very personal and I have left them for later. But later has arrived, as we hit the halfway mark. So, I will trust the process and honour my commitment. I said, at the outset, that I was doing this for myself. I could not have anticipated the many gifts that it would bring me.

I have not learned these lessons in a vacuum. Many posts include people who have given me permission to name them and to tell their stories. My gratitude for the friendship, love, support and lessons that these relationships have brought me is immeasurable.

> Tell the truth and tell it faster.
> Whatever the outcome, at least you
> will be dealing with reality.

* * *

LESSON 11: TELL THE TRUTH FASTER (TTTF)

In 1999, Kevin, my partner at the time, was diagnosed with full-blown AIDS.[27] He skipped HIV and went straight to the bottom of life's pulse – he was literally dying. Lying in a public hospital the day before his thirty-fifth birthday, Kevin told me that his father – who lived out of town – would be visiting him the following day. "Are you going to tell him?" I asked. "I'll tell him when I get out," was his reply. I looked at him – all forty kilograms of him – and said, "You won't get out *until* you tell him." He did tell his father, and their relationship became one of the forces that contributed to his healing. In this little anecdote about Kevin and his father, lies today's lesson. It is the cliché of all clichés: *The truth will set you free.*

I am adding *time* to this adage. How long will you wait before you tell the truth, and what price will you pay for not telling it? When I look back on my life and the many times that I found myself in a predicament, I can trace the cause of my troubles to my not telling the truth quickly enough. I knew I was gay, yet I prolonged coming out. Much pain and suffering could have been avoided had I told the absolute truth – faster. I accepted a job as a Jewish Studies teacher – so that I could get residency papers for Australia. I lasted three days! The road there was memorable, and I had the time of my life – but I ignored the little voice that was whispering ("this is wrong") to me. I delayed telling the truth, and it cost me my reputation and left those who had employed me bewildered, with egg on their face.

---

[27] This disclosure has been made at the request, and with the permission, of Kevin Lowe. I am eternally grateful for the lessons I learned with him and am sorry for the pain that accompanied many of the lessons.

Because I now live by **Lesson 1 (TTP)**, I seldom regret my choices. Each choice has led me perfectly to my next destination. There is no doubt, however, that truth-telling makes the entire process so much simpler. One of the greatest aphorisms, found in Shakespeare's *Hamlet*, is spoken by Polonius as his last piece of advice to his son:

> *This above all: to thine own self be true, And it must follow, as the night the day, Thou canst not then be false to any man.*

Being true to yourself means that the first person to whom we need to tell the truth is ourselves. Truly knowing oneself means that you tell yourself the truth about yourself. What do you know? Who needs to know? What are you not willing to look at, honestly and truthfully? You cannot change anything until you accept it. How will you change if you are not accepting what needs to be changed? How will you change if you are not telling the truth about it?

And what about the people around you? What do they need to know? What are you not saying? How many conversations are you having in your head, thinking that they will hear you by some magic osmotic process? Others cannot hear our thoughts, yet we tell ourselves things so many times that – eventually – we forget that we haven't even told the person who needed to hear these thoughts in the first place. This is called magical thinking. It results in passive-aggressive behaviour – the worst kind of behaviour! If you find yourself punishing yourself – or others – in covert and subtle ways, the chances are it is because a truth needs to be told. So, tell that truth, and tell it faster. Whatever the outcome, at least you will be dealing with reality. When we deal with what *is*, we can take action. You cannot take action from a place of denial. Why would you? But when you stare reality in the face and speak from your heart, you allow yourself – and others – to take action.

TELL THE TRUTH FASTER – LOCKDOWN DAY 11 (PART 2)

Some pundits believe that the discovery of the coronavirus was kept hidden, and that a quicker telling of the truth could have prevented its spread. I don't know whether this is true or not, but, if it is, we are seeing the devastating consequences of not telling the truth fast enough. The Buddhists have a beautiful concept called Dharma – it is Karma's lesser-known twin. Karma is what we bring from a past life into this one. Dharma is more interesting. Its literal translation is 'that which saves'. Brandon Bays defines Dharma slightly differently. She says that it is "the right action in the present moment". When you tell the truth faster, you become open to Dharma. You allow yourself to discern the correct action for now. It is truth-telling of the highest order.

TTTF is a tough lesson for this time. Often, the right action for the present moment is to tell the truth. Sometimes it is to keep quiet. In our personal lives, this may not necessarily be the time for telling the truth faster to others. But for me, as I said yesterday, some truths are coming up which I can't ignore. So, perhaps, TTTF is just about quietly acknowledging to yourself whatever truths this time is revealing to you. And then to trust that, when the time is right, you will follow your Dharma and take the right action for that moment. Happy truth day!

LESSON 12
PLAY IN THE LIGHT

Darkness cannot drive out darkness; only light can do that. Hate cannot drive out hate; only love can do that.
— MARTIN LUTHER KING, JR.

Healthy things do not grow in the dark. Mould, spores and fungi thrive in dark environments, but flowers, trees, fruit and vegetables all require sunshine. You will not find the kind of growth you want in secret, shady places. Even nightshades – a particular type of plant that flowers in the dark – require sunlight.[28] That is the bottom line.

But what does that mean in practice, and how do you apply that to your life? Allow me to digress slightly and be somewhat controversial – I trust that what I have to say will be interpreted positively. The HI virus that causes AIDS was first detected in the West among homosexual men. Homosexuality was forbidden – and illegal – in most places in the world. Gay people were literally forced to live their lives in secret – in the dark, as it were. Homosexuals were not allowed to play in the light: shame and self-loathing were, for a long time, a part of what it meant to be gay in the world. Sadly, in many countries of the world, this is still the case. Is it any surprise that the

---
28 Adapted from www.levilusko.com

deadly virus originated in a sector of the population that was forced to stay in the dark?

Louise Hay began working with gay men when the AIDS pandemic hit the USA. This is what she had to say:

> *When you're talking about the disease called AIDS, I find you're really dealing with people who have a lot of self-hatred. They feel they're not good enough. There's a lot of resentment towards their families, and very often there's been a lifestyle that's been very abusive for the body. They've not taken loving care of themselves and when this gets turned around, healing takes place.* [29]

As a gay man, I have had my share of self-esteem issues to deal with in my life. I have always had mixed feelings about the 'coming out' process. On the one hand, you come out into the light. On the other hand, the very act of definition puts you into a new 'box'. It fills me with much joy that many younger people, whom I encounter these days, do not feel the need to define or box themselves as 'gay' or 'straight'. While some people decry (or do not understand) the LGBTQI+ initialism, for me it represents a movement away from the dark and into the light. You can be whatever you want, and you can be proud of it! There are a few extreme positions in this regard and I am still making my mind up about some of it. But, nowadays, in many parts of the world (sadly, not enough), people are afforded the opportunity to feel a sense of self-worth just for being who they are – not labelled or categorised. I love this. This is playing in the

---

[29] www.latimes.com/archives/la-xpm-1988-03-02-vw-213-story.html

LESSON 12: PLAY IN THE LIGHT

light. My humanity makes me worthy of self-respect and the respect of others – not my label or my actions.

Often, when we are not telling the truth, it is because we are in denial. Martha Beck provides the following useful questions for "clearing denial":

- What am I afraid to know?
- What am I hiding?
- What do I almost know?
- What knowledge am I avoiding? [30]

> **Share of yourself openly, let people in, connect with your dark side and subject it to the light of day.**

When you play in the light, and reveal whatever it is you are hiding, you are exercising your own "coming out". Sometimes, shame or guilt may be preventing you from playing in the light. But shame and guilt are terrible emotions with which to live permanently. In my experience, many people are more accepting than we think and the feeling of liberation that comes with no longer having to live with the crippling feelings of shame and guilt are worth the temporary pain. You regain your self-worth and, in time, you give yourself the gift of self-esteem. It

---

[30] Martha Beck, *When Is It Okay to Lie?* in O, The Oprah Magazine, 2014. www.oprah.com/inspiration/when-to-lie-when-to-tell-the-truth/all

is impossible to play in the light without accepting and honouring your own worthiness; you are worthy of love, joy, success, abundance, and whatever else you wish for.

You owe it to yourself to come out of the shadow of unworthiness. We don't walk, by accident, into a wonderful life. We have to commit to playing in the light, to decide what we stand for, and to be prepared for other people's reactions. As Kamal Ravikant puts it:

> *It begins by looking inside ourselves, because when it rises from within, we have no choice but to express it, to live it. That is when the magic happens: fulfilment, happiness, relationships, and success.* [31]

The oft-misunderstood African philosophy of ubuntu ("A person is a person through other persons") also comes to mind in this lesson. Archbishop Desmond Tutu famously described ubuntu as meaning, "My humanity is caught up, is inextricably bound up, in what is yours." It is very hard to practise ubuntu if you are hiding away, or if your actions are forcing another to hide away. Ubuntu requires a certain "coming out" – almost an expression of "I am OK; you are OK". Playing in the light, like ubuntu, means that I allow myself to be seen. And, in asking you to see me, I see you. Interestingly, South Africa's Truth and Reconciliation Commission, which was led by Tutu, was founded on this principle. Playing in the light requires truth-telling – as per **Lesson 11 (TTTF)**. Once the truth is told, we get to "play" – to lighten up, be child-like and celebrate our authentic selves. Share of yourself openly, let people in, connect with your dark side and subject it to the light of day.

---

[31] Kamal Ravikant, *Live Your Truth*, self-published 2013.

LESSON 12: PLAY IN THE LIGHT

This lesson is best encapsulated by Rumi, one of my favourite poets of all time:

If you want the moon, do not hide at night;
If you want a rose, do not run from the thorns;
If you want love…
do not hide from yourself

> **You owe it to yourself to come out of the shadow of unworthiness.**

PLAY IN THE LIGHT – LOCKDOWN DAY 12

I learned something based on feedback I received about yesterday's Lesson (TTTF). In the post, I focused on the person who needs to tell the truth. What I neglected is the effect that our *not* telling the truth fast enough has on the people around us. In my life, I have hurt some exceptionally good people by being afraid to tell the truth quickly enough. Being lied to (whether actively or by omission) can have devastating consequences for others. Having been made aware of this 'blind spot', I have apologised to some very dear people who have suffered as a result of my lack of courage to tell the truth fast enough.

* * *

Martin Luther King (quoted above) says that love and light drive out hatred and darkness. Pesach, which Jews all over the world are preparing to celebrate, is the festival of freedom. The way we celebrate that freedom is by gathering together with our loved ones. At the Pesach table, children are given pride of place. The youngest child sings a song, children hunt for buried treasure (the 'Afikomen'), and the book we read from contains many songs for children and parents to sing together.

> We don't walk, by accident, into a wonderful life.

One Rabbi goes so far as to say that "Passover celebrates love". Another describes it as the festival when the Jews "fell in love with God and committed ourselves to one another."

When I originally conceived this lesson, the light referred to the truth, but I think that at this time, on the Eve of Pesach and Easter, the light is as much about love as it is about truth. Tonight, for the first time in living memory, I will not spend Pesach with my family. All over the world, families will not be together for Pesach and Easter this year. Every year, I complain about Pesach – I'm not a big fan. And yet, today, I would do anything to be able to spend it with my family, surrounded by the love and the light that family brings.

I am being careful not to say, "After this is over, I will never …", but what I do know for sure is that I will never again take a family gathering for granted. Rather than complain about the hassle of gathering, the prayers that go on for too long, or my dislike for matza, I will look up from my pettiness and focus on the love of family and the light of the candles.

Lockdown has brought a certain darkness (loneliness, fear, anxiety). The blessing is that I can now see the light that I had and may not have appreciated. Rather than focus tonight on who is not there and how I wish it could be different, when I light my candles and say my prayers, I will give thanks for the light of times past and pray for the light of times to come.

LESSON 13
CHOOSE AGAIN

One day you will wake up and there won't be any more time to do the things you've always wanted. Do it now.
— PAULO COELHO

At some point in my life, I decided that I wanted to live in Australia. My sister was already living there, and she was in the process of applying for citizenship. I decided that if she was going to be there, I wanted to be there too.

One day, while on holiday in Israel, I revisited my alma mater – the Hebrew University of Jerusalem – where I saw a sign for a 'Senior Educators Programme in Jewish Education'. "Wow!" I thought to myself, "That would be a great way to get into Australia." I applied, I was accepted, and so began one of the most incredible years of my life. I was paid to study and meet wonderful people from all over the world while spending a year in one of my favourite cities. Although I was interested in Jewish Education, I did not obey **Lesson 11 (TTTF)**. I had a hidden agenda – I wanted to get to Australia.

The Universe listened to me – I was offered a job as a high school Jewish Studies teacher in Melbourne. I was asked to begin my job by accompanying a group of twenty Grade 10 students on a three-month trip to Israel.

Life could not have been better – a job in Australia and a three-month paid 'vacation' back in Israel to kick-start my new life. I had the time of my life for those three months. The kids were great. We toured the whole of Israel, and I could not have been happier. We returned to Melbourne in early January, and I moved in with my very good friend Ruth who was only too happy to have me as a flatmate.

On 5 February 1999, I began my job as a high school Jewish Studies teacher. There was only one problem: I wasn't a high school Jewish Studies teacher. I knew by second break on the first day that I had made a mistake. I was so focused on my goal (i.e. getting there), that I had never given any thought to what the other side might actually look like. It might sound strange, but I honestly believed that I could 'fake it 'till I made it'. Unfortunately, I could not. Arriving home that afternoon, I told Ruth that I wanted to quit. She thought I was mad, as did the Principal when I informed him on day two of my new job that I wished to quit. He thought I was having a nervous breakdown. He offered me counselling and implored me to give it time. But I knew deep in my heart that I did not want to be a high school teacher in Melbourne. I wanted out.

I returned to the school that Wednesday with a heavy heart. I did not even finish the day. I left at second break. I packed my bag, and I left. I walked out of the school and kept walking. My apartment was very far away from the school, but I did not take a bus. I walked, and I walked, and I walked. I knew that the only choice left to me was to choose again.

LESSON 13: CHOOSE AGAIN

And so, I did. Deep inside me, I felt a calling to return to South Africa. I decided to leave Australia and return home. Of course I could have stayed. Who knows, things may have gotten better – but, having made what I perceived to be the wrong choice, I chose to make a new choice. I chose not to suffer the anxiety of uncertainty but rather to call it – and call it quickly. Some may see this behaviour as irrational and impulsive, but it was not: 'Impulse' is a synonym for 'instinct'. And instinct – that feeling of "knowing" that emanates from deep in the gut – is not a rational thing; it's the polar opposite.

> Once the choice is made, you give life a chance to come to your aid.

Within two months of returning to South Africa, I had a post at a primary school, teaching children whom I loved and who loved me. I met Simone – the "hooter" I spoke about earlier – at the school, and she went on to become one of my best friends. Three months later I met my partner, Kevin. Two years later, my sister and her family returned to live in South Africa. My choice had paid off. It had been the right thing to do. I chose once, and it was the wrong choice. I chose again, and this time it was the right choice. Had it not been, I would have chosen again.

This lesson is not suggesting that choices and decisions do not require thought and consideration. And I am not advocating for impulsivity, especially when it comes to decisions that are potentially life-changing. Rather, this lesson is an antidote to procrastination. Procrastination seldom changes anything. Ancient Greek philosophers developed a word to describe procrastination, "Akrasia".[32] Akrasia is the state of acting against your better judgement. It is when you do one thing (or nothing) even though you know you should be making a different choice. "I'll think about it" is often just another way of saying, "I don't want to make the choice I know I need to make." If you know that no amount of "thinking about it" is going to change anything, rather just make the choice. As I have said previously, the universe supports action. Once the choice is made, you give life a chance to come to your aid.

> **Procrastination seldom changes anything.**

There are great similarities between this rule and the previous one of non-attachment. A wise friend once told me to "make your decisions easily" – I love that. If

---

[32] www.jamesclear.com

you think or feel that something is not 'right', don't feel the need to suffer endlessly. You chose once, so choose again. Do it as quickly and as easily as possible. Don't misunderstand me. This is not about giving up. This is about one of two things: You've given it your all, and it's still not working; or, at your deepest level – call it gut instinct – you know that something is not right. The grass may not be greener on the other side, but that is no reason to stay where the grass feels wrong. Choose new grass. Sometimes the right choice is simply to make a new choice. Happy choosing!

CHOOSE AGAIN - LOCKDOWN DAY 13

For many of us, where we find ourselves during lockdown is a result of choices made along the way. My current circumstances are a direct result of conscious and difficult choices made at the end of 2019 / early 2020. There were a few "choose agains", made with absolutely no idea that we were weeks away from a global pandemic and lockdown. I have no idea whether I would have made different choices, had I known. For me, that is irrelevant. We make our choices based on the information we have at the time. How it then unfolds is how it unfolds.

Regret, like worry, is a waste of time for me. Lockdown is, however, forcing me to do some mental housekeeping – to evaluate some of my choices, to take responsibility for them and, most importantly, to make peace with them. "It is as it is; it is as it is; it is as it is." This has become almost a daily mantra for me.

"And now what?" I find myself asking. My deep and very personal sense about Covid-19 is that it has broken the illusion that we have an endless supply of time. If I have one regret, it is that I procrastinated. I never visited my sick aunt, who is now locked down in an old age home. Will I see her again? Why didn't I make time in 2019 BC? I never made peace with a friend, never picking up the phone just to say sorry. It feels too late and, even though it's not, I still haven't chosen again.

> The grass may not be greener on the other side, but that is no reason to stay where the grass feels wrong. Choose again.

There is no going back. Life will never go 'back to normal'. I think we're in something akin to the Industrial Revolution. Life never went back to normal afterwards. What my life looks like after this Revolution has a lot to do with the choices I need to make.

Where do I want to live? I'm going to allow myself to choose again. How do I want to live? I'm already making some new choices. What work don't I want to do any more? Those choices are bubbling under the

LESSON 13: CHOOSE AGAIN

surface. Now that I have made conscious peace with the fact that my time here is finite, my biggest commitment to myself is to make choices that serve me – and to make them more quickly than I would have in the past. For me, Lockdown Time is Choices Time. Happy choosing!

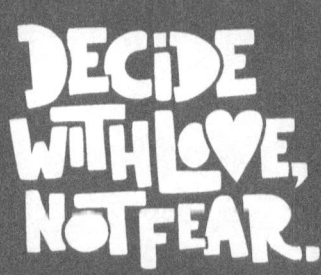

LESSON 14

DECIDE WITH LOVE, NOT FEAR

*When you make a choice,
you change the future.*

— DEEPAK CHOPRA

In **Lesson 11 (TTTF)**, I mentioned Kevin who, when he was diagnosed as HIV positive, already had full-blown AIDS. His recovery had as much to do with medication as it had to do with a decision he had to make. Lying in a state hospital, surrounded by the love of family and friends, he had what is known as a near-death experience (NDE). NDEs have been explained in many ways – some take a scientific approach, while others take a religious or transcendent approach. Either way, for those who experience an NDE, it is as real as any experience that we have in our waking states. This is the story he recounted when he was well, and out of hospital.[33]

> One day, soon after being admitted to hospital, Kevin opened his eyes to see an old man standing at his bedside. He did not recognise him, but he knew him – if that makes any sense. The man told Kevin that he would return and that when he came back, Kevin would need to decide whether he wanted to live or die – either choice would be acceptable. The only condition the man placed on the choice was that he was to make the decision with love – not fear. True to his word, the old man returned a few weeks later. Kevin had a visitor at the time, and, in his semi-delirious state, he told her to switch off the TV – but there was no television in the room!

---

[33] Told with Kevin's permission.

In that moment, he found himself surrounded by people, and suddenly the old man was back. "It's time," he said.

When Kevin relayed the story afterwards, he told us that, as he weighed his decision, he realised that he was not yet done with love. It was as simple as that. His illness had brought him closer to his father, his partner, and his many friends and family, all of whom had rallied around to support his recovery. "I hadn't finished loving," were his words. Kevin decided to choose life. He did not choose life because he was scared of the other side – in fact he remains totally unafraid of death to this day. He chose life because he was not done with love yet. The people went away, and his decision propelled him to health and wellness. The road was long, with the medication certainly playing its part, but the point is that he had to decide to live. Over and above this, he had to make his decision from a place of love, rather than a place of fear.

> **When you face a big decision, listen to your heart and make your choices from a place of love.**

You will have many decisions to make in your life. Please use this story to guide you. Don't do things because you are scared of what may or may not happen. When you face a big decision, listen to your heart, and make your decisions from a place of love. Generally, when I decide with love, I find that I am more response-able and,

LESSON 14: DECIDE WITH LOVE, NOT FEAR

when I decide with fear, I tend to be reactive. It's such a cliché, but love really is a better motivator than fear.

Gary Zukav, the author of *Seat of the Soul*, the book which Oprah Winfrey describes as her greatest influence (what high praise!), expresses it most beautifully:

> *Feel your intentions in your heart. Feel not what your mind tells you, but what your heart tells you. Rather than serve the fake gods of your mind, serve your heart, the real God. You will not find God in your intellect. Divine Intelligence is in the heart.* [34]

When you start to see your decisions as lying somewhere on the love-fear continuum, the decision-making process becomes much simpler. Tony Robbins[35] describes decisions as being the "doorway to change" and goes on to say that a real decision can only be measured by taking action. When I left my corporate job to work for myself, I cannot say I wasn't terrified. With meagre savings and only a vague plan, I made a decision to love myself enough to take my life back. The daily grind of employment was taking its toll and I knew that I wanted to do something bigger with my life. My mother implored me to stay employed: "You're a middle-aged white man. Stay in your job!" Of course, her worries were based on love for me but, ultimately, listening to her would have meant succumbing to fear. I decided with love, for myself, and have not looked back. When you work out what is important to you, the process of deciding with love, not fear, becomes so much easier.

Electing to listen to the voices of fear, whether external or internal, prevents life from sending new opportunities.

---

[34] Gary Zukav, *The Seat of the Soul*, Simon & Schuster, 1989.

[35] American author, coach, speaker and philanthropist.

I was amazed at how my network 'appeared' after I decided with love. It had always been there, but fear had prevented me from seeing it or tapping into it. Whatever your fear – disappointing someone, not being 'good enough', or being judged – I urge you to decide with love.

Stephanie Dankelson[36] provides this useful checklist for deciding with love, rather than fear:

- What are my options?
- Which one is based on fear – which one is based on love for myself?
- What is it that I am afraid of (that would lead me to make the fear-based decision)?
- What would the love-based decision do for me?
- What is the best thing that could happen with this scenario?
- What is the worst thing that could happen? So what? (See **Lesson 13, Choose Again.**)

A Course in Miracles[37] expresses the purpose of this lesson beautifully:

> *All healing is essentially a release from fear.*

DECIDE WITH LOVE, NOT FEAR – LOCKDOWN DAY 14

Today, twenty-seven years ago, Chris Hani was assassinated, by people who chose fear rather than love. South Africa stood on the brink of anarchy. Were fear and hate going to win as we edged closer towards democracy? That night Nelson Mandela, who was a year away from becoming our President, went on TV and addressed the nation. Some say that was the moment he became the

---

[36] www.stephanie-dankelson.com

[37] www.acim.org

LESSON 14: DECIDE WITH LOVE, NOT FEAR

leader of us all. Mandela could have used the assassination to galvanise a revolution. People wanted revenge. Instead, he chose a message of love:

> *Now is the time for all South Africans to stand together against those who ... wish to destroy what Chris Hani gave his life for – the freedom of all of us ... When we, as one people, act together decisively, with discipline and determination, nothing can stop us.*

How ironic that, in his latest speech, President Ramaphosa sent us the same message. I believe that both Mandela and Ramaphosa's messages are messages of love – stand together, love yourself and others enough to stay home, take precautions, help each other, help the less fortunate, and sacrifice a portion of your salary if you can.

The extension of our lockdown, while expected, caused unease. It is easy to let fear take over. But, as this lesson teaches, the opposite of fear is love. We don't have to make choices from a place of fear. I stay home, not because of fear, but because of love – love for myself, love for others, love for life. I don't want fear to win.

Of course, today is also Good Friday. The New Testament, describing Jesus's crucifixion, says: "Greater love has no one than this, that he lay down his life for his friends." We are all being called upon to make sacrifices now. It empowers me when I see these sacrifices as acts of love rather than fear. Today, I'm recommitting to making my choices from a place of love. I hope you will too.

LESSON 15
READ THE SIGNS

Signs don't shout; they whisper.
— A.D. POSEY

Remember that course that led me to a year of study in Israel? I found the course while walking through the corridors of my University – I saw a sign and I followed it. Life is full of signs and signals – the key is to notice them. In my case, it was a literal sign that changed the course of my life. The fact that it did not work out as I imagined is not the point: not only did it provide me with great experiences; it also taught me invaluable lessons. The secret is to 'notice'.

'Notice' is a great word because, in English, a notice is, quite literally, a sign. Of course, the majority of things that we need to notice don't come in the form of a literal sign, but, when we are awake and not sleepwalking through life, we begin to notice – we become aware of the signs, and we begin to trust ourselves enough to give attention to what is going on in our life. [38]

Life is speaking to us all the time. The questions we need to ask are: "What is it saying?" and "Am I listening?" Our home was burgled a few years ago. Thankfully, the

---

[38] I did a workshop called "More to Life", which is run by the Kairos Foundation of South Africa (KFSA). At the front of the room, on either side of the boards, were two signs that said 'NOTICE'. I learned the power of "noticing" at this workshop, and am eternally grateful for that, and all the other lessons that More to Life, and my time on the KFSA Board, taught me. Check out www.moretolife.org.

robbers did not get into the house, but they did manage to steal things from outside our house. We reflected on the fact that our security needed an upgrade, but we left it at that. Two nights later, the burglars returned. This time, our dogs heard them and barked, and we managed to chase the burglars away. Only then were we sufficiently freaked out to stop procrastinating and take action – we secured the gate, fixed the broken garage door, and sorted out the alarm system.

The first burglary was a sign, but we ignored it. Life was not having any of that. "You want to ignore the warning sign?" it seemed to ask; "That's fine, I'll send you another. Perhaps this time, you'll listen!" And we did listen. Had we swung into action after the first sign, the second burglary would probably not have happened. Another sign from life was necessary. That is how it is with signs – when we don't listen to the whisper, life sends us a shout. Sometimes, life is shouting at us and we're still not listening. Some signs may bring a deep knowing and a feeling that we are on the right track (this is sometimes called 'flow'). Others are a sign to wake up and get our act together.

The Swiss psychotherapist, Carl Jung, popularised the term 'synchronicity', which he defined as 'meaningful coincidences'. I love that definition. For Jung, synchronicity was how he defined a situation where two or more seemingly random signs are actually connected – not by cause, but by meaning. The trick is to notice the connection and to find its meaning. Not everything is a sign, however, and sometimes 'shit happens'. I used to think everything had meaning. When I got a sore throat,

I would soul-search about what I needed to be expressing (à la Louise Hay). My doctor – a man of science who doesn't believe in signs – once said to me, "Trevor, there are goggas (insects) in the air." He was correct: sometimes, it just is what it is.

As I said in a previous post, we need to find a balance between randomness ('shit happens') and meaning ('signs are everywhere'). The trick is not to give in, either to randomness – where nothing has meaning, or to synchronicity – where everything is over-analysed. People who see it all as random are victims – they don't realise that their behaviour and actions are contributing to what is happening in their lives. They are ignoring life's feedback. Conversely, people who see signs everywhere may get into analysis paralysis.

I prefer a middle ground that errs on the side of seeing connections between things. Life wants us to pay attention. It sends its signs for free, but if we ignore them, the cost may be high.

READ THE SIGNS - LOCKDOWN DAY 15

If ever there was a sign that we all need to slow down, the Covid-19 pandemic is it. In 2019 BC, I left it to the Greta Thunbergs of this world to worry about climate change and how we were destroying the natural world. Now we see that, as human activity slows down, the natural world is coming back to itself. The internet is full of beautiful pictures and videos of animals returning to places that humans have deserted, and skies no longer filled with pollution. As it is in nature, so too can it be in my life. Freed of the 'busy-ness', I can slow down and notice things about myself and my life. There is time and space to read the signs. What is working in my life? What is not working? What have I failed to notice? What am I noticing now? What am I going to do about it? These are crucial questions.

> ### Life wants us to pay attention.

In my own life, the signs are positive – I'm relatively healthy, connecting with people, still getting work – and I'm earning money. I have a confession to make: I'm quite enjoying lockdown. I like the quiet. I like the slow pace of my daily life. At the same time, I am acutely aware that many people are suffering. But even as we prepare for an unknown future, I am choosing to believe that some good will come out of Covid-19. Hopefully, we will realise that rampant capitalism and greed do not serve humanity. The 'free market' is hardly free. Look at the price we're paying. We will slow down, notice more, and care more about the things that matter – family, friends, touch, connection.

Some say I have a "Pollyanna" view of life. I think they are right. What I am grappling with now is how to find a balance between my optimism and reading the signs for what they are. The signs seem to indicate that things will get worse and that this won't go away quickly, so I am mentally preparing myself for the fact that life will never

LESSON 15: READ THE SIGNS

be the same. Rather than resisting it, I am leaning into it. I don't want to go back to 'normal'. Normal brought us here. I want to read the signs that self-gratification is not the way to live.

The poor matter. Earth matters. We all matter.[39]

Richard Carlson, who wrote *Don't Sweat the Small Stuff*, says:

> *Everything has God's fingerprints on it ... the fact that we can't see the beauty in something doesn't suggest that it's not there. Rather, it suggests that we are not looking carefully enough or with a broad enough perspective to see it.* [40]

For me, reading the signs at this time is about looking more carefully and more broadly. It is about erring on the side of optimism while staying realistic – tricky, I know, but I'm working it out too.

Happy Noticing Day. I pray that all our signs will be more positive than negative, more optimistic than pessimistic, and more hopeful than hopeless.[41]

---

[39] After lockdown, I was blessed to work with a group of entrepreneurs in rural KwaZulu-Natal. Of the many things I taught them, the phrase "You matter!" was the one that stuck with them. I have subsequently created a personal development course called "I Matter!" which captures the essence of the lessons. Underneath all the lessons lies a simple truth. Each one of us is a person of significance; our existence matters. If I matter, you matter. We all matter.

[40] Richard Carlson, *Don't Sweat the Small Stuff... and it's all Small Stuff*, Hodder & Stoughton, 1998.

[41] As we appeared to be coming out of the pandemic, Putin invaded Ukraine. As I revisit this book, in preparation for publishing this edition, I am sorry to say that I am not sure we have learned much. I remain an optimistic person but the signs I am seeing are definitely stretching my optimism! Nonetheless, I prefer to focus on the signs in my immediate life, rather than the headlines!

LESSON 16
BE KIND

No matter how educated, talented, rich or cool you believe you are, how you treat people ultimately tells all.

— UNKNOWN

I would like to preface this piece with two notes:
- In post-apartheid South Africa, we use the term 'K-word' to refer to an obnoxious and extremely hurtful word used by racists to describe black people during apartheid. In this piece, which describes my experience growing up during apartheid, I have used the letter 'K' to refer to the word, because I refuse to type it out here and give it power. Its use was cruel, and its intention unkind.
- Sections of this post were used in a piece I was commissioned to write for the book *I love you I hate you*, based on the 'Love Jozi' range of T-shirts. [42]

This lesson follows on closely from **Lesson 7 (Practise Patience)**, particularly in your dealings with other people. At my fortieth birthday party, my dearest childhood friend, Lael, described me as 'kind' and went on to talk about the virtues of this trait. Now, just over ten years later, I smile when I think of her choice of kindness

---

[42] www.lovejozi.com

as my overarching personal quality. I wear the label of kindness proudly. I like being kind. Kindness comes naturally to me. It may be because I was the victim of a lot of cruelty growing up. I bore witness to a great deal of unkindness being doled out to others too.

> Sometimes, kindness is just about seeing the other person, and acknowledging their existence.

Growing up in a time of great machismo and racism influenced my life – first negatively, and then positively. The negative part was obviously the actual experience. I was not born with a macho gene – I was apparently not in that line. I really don't do the whole 'be a man' thing very well. My dad, as fate would have it, was a quintessential man of his time – loud, boorish and racist. He did not want a 'soft' son, and he certainly did not want an anti-apartheid son. In fact, when I was young, I thought Joe Slovo was a long-lost relative as my dad would often refer to him as "your uncle".

As I recount in the preface, I grew up in a residential hotel in a "poor white" area of Johannesburg. The hotel had a large backyard. Every day after lunch, I would take my school bag and go to the ironing room to say hello to

LESSON 16: BE KIND

Thelma, who was always there, ironing away. Thelma was large, with a laugh to match, and a voice that bubbled. She would sing as she ironed, and I would begin to do my homework – sometimes on the floor, other times on an upturned beer crate. Everything happened in the yard. It was in the yard that the cooks, the waiters and the cleaners could relax. Off duty or on a break, away from the ever-watchful eyes and endless demands of their white taskmasters, they could breathe – and so could I. The white people made me nervous; the black people made me happy. It sounds so silly now to say things like that, but that is how it was for me then. The white people tried so hard all the time. They were always *trying* to be funny, or clever, or friendly, but they weren't really any of those things – they were just loud, cruel, rude – and silly, especially with the servants. The servants always pretended to find them funny – I guess they didn't really have a choice. Apartheid made it difficult for anybody to be themselves.

One day, Jimmy – an obnoxious, exceptionally large man – brought a rubber snake to the dining room. As David, the waiter, brought him a menu, he pulled the snake out from under the tablecloth. David was, of course, terrified of snakes. As he jumped and screamed, the entire table roared with laughter. I just didn't get it – what was so funny about embarrassing a grown-up in front of so many people? I didn't laugh. And, of course, Jimmy noticed. I hated Jimmy. He would always chase me. Even though he could never catch me, I found him scary. Whenever Jimmy was in the dining room, I would take my lunch into the yard. "You going to your 'K' friends?" he asked me one day. "Watch out for them," he jeered, "You turn around, and they'll stab you in the back."

The fact that my 'K' friends were within earshot of his voice was of little consequence to Jimmy or any of the other men who liberally bandied the word about. I don't know when I first knew that it was a bad word – I just knew. My 'K' friends were never rude to me. But, more than anything, they *saw* me. They called me 'Clever Trevor', and never teased or mocked me. In the yard, kindness was doled out freely. Interestingly, almost all the people there were of Zulu heritage. I learned, years later, that the Zulu greeting, 'Sawubona', literally means 'I see you'. Sometimes, kindness is just about seeing the other person, and acknowledging their existence. In the yard, I was seen, and I learned kindness from people who had so little kindness bestowed upon them.

My friend David's mom, Pam, taught me the old adage that says, "You catch more flies with honey than you do with vinegar." I draw upon this wisdom often. Treating people with kindness is not only compassionate – it is also respectful, collaborative and productive. People respond well to kindness. They are invariably more engaged and open when they feel acknowledged and respected. If you find yourself needing to have a difficult conversation with someone, approach them from a place of kindness, rather than with judgement or animosity. Your chances of resolving the matter equitably will be far greater.

As mentioned earlier, I encourage my clients to add a 'random act of kindness' to their daily rituals. Sometimes, the kindness is for others; other times it is about being kinder to themselves. Either way, an act of kindness releases the feel-good hormones (dopamine, oxytocin and serotonin). Being kind has been proven to help boost the immune system and reduce blood pressure, as well as reduce stress and anxiety.[43]

Kindness connects us with others – compassion, empathy and generosity make us feel better about ourselves, while making others feel better too. The "psychological bliss" that we feel, after an act of kindness, is akin to taking a drug and has led researchers to coin the phrase "helper's high" – a unique physical sensation that results from helping others.[44]

BE KIND - LOCKDOWN DAY 16

Week three – and another two weeks of this … I shudder to think about what is happening in some households now as tempers fray, liquor dries up, cigarettes become contraband, children get bored, parents buckle under the pressure of home-schooling, and home-style haircuts make us look like aliens. If ever there was a time for kindness, this week is it. But what exactly does it mean to be kind? Kindness in action is really compassion. And, once again, I will defer to the wisdom of Brandon Bays, who defines compassion as "kindness over rightness".

I think that is the way we all get to be kind this week: we forego our rightness. We let other people be, and we ask that they let us be. Rather than sitting in judgement, we sit in kindness. When David, my friend mentioned above, experiences me as being judgemental, he simply says, 'Judy!' (referring to 'Judge Judy'). That is his shorthand

---

[43] www.myfoothold.org

[44] www.buzzfeed.com

way of letting me know I'm being judgemental, and that kindness may be a better option. Let's leave judgement to the judges. Let's replace it with words of kindness and acts of compassion.

> I learned kindness from people who had so little kindness bestowed on them.

We need to extend kindness not only to others but also to ourselves. We're all taking strain. In fact, as I write this post, I am reflecting on how tired I am. This post may even feel a bit strained. You know what? That's okay. I trust that I am writing for kind people, and I'm being kind to myself, lowering the high standards I set for myself to be profound and word-perfect every day. I would urge you to do the same for yourselves. Lower some of those self-imposed high standards. It's Day sixteen. It's okay to feel a bit 'over it all'. Let's just be careful not to take those frustrations out on our loved ones. Let's be kind to each other and ourselves.

My final point today is a bit of a soapbox moment. I want to say something about the 'home-schooling' pressure that has descended upon the world. Although I don't have children, I taught for a long time and am still involved in the development of learning materials for school children. Please apply the 'Be kind' lesson to

LESSON 16: BE KIND

your kids. There are so many ways to learn – and so many things to learn about – that are not in the 'curriculum'.

I understand that school is important, but I also know that the world existed for a long time before there were schools and curricula. Don't be too hard on your kids – and don't be too hard on yourselves either – you're not qualified teachers, and it's damn hard to be both schoolteacher and parent. Just be parents. There are so many things you can teach your kids now, that don't exist in the curriculum. Above all, you can teach them, by your example, how to be kind and compassionate. They will learn more from that than from online learning.

Happy Kindness Day!

LESSON 17
SHOW UP

Eighty percent of success is showing up.
— WOODY ALLEN

On 21 January 2009, a strange-looking woman walked onto the stage at the Scottish Exhibition and Conference Centre in Glasgow for an audition on *Britain's Got Talent*. She had a horrible hairstyle, an awful dress, and looked far too old to be on the show. Everyone in the audience was laughing at her when she said that she wanted to be like Elaine Paige – until she opened her mouth to sing. In November of that year, Susan Boyle's debut album, *I Dreamed a Dream*, was the most pre-ordered album of all time on Amazon!

On that morning in January when Susan got up, she had every reason in the world not to attend the audition. A middle-aged unmarried woman who lived alone with her cat, and who had only ever sung in church choirs and her local pub – her nerves must have been shot. I have little doubt that she had moments of "I'm not doing this" – but she did. She boarded a bus, she risked humiliation and rejection, but Susan showed up. Had she decided not to get on the bus, she would probably still be sitting in her house with her cat, dreaming of what could have been. But Susan said "Yes" to life. She knew that she had a calling and she followed her calling. But the fulfilment of her life's dream started with the smallest of steps – buying a bus ticket! There is no doubt that Susan had the talent to match her dream to make it come true, but that's not the point. The point is that she showed up. She gave it her best. The audience was on their feet within minutes of hearing her angelic voice. It is one of my favourite clips to watch. Google "Susan Boyle Audition" to watch it.

> Answer the phone. Buy the ticket. Get on the bus – you never know where the journey will take you.

You will be invited to many things in your life – parties, meetings and events. More often than not, you will have something else to do – a reason not to go and an excuse to say no. Don't! As much as possible – and wherever possible – if life invites you, it wants you to say "Yes". When I reflect upon the path my life has taken, so many of the most important relationships and events of my life have been a result of simply *showing up*. I did not have to do anything else for life to open the next door. Had I not shown up, however, the door would not have opened.

I found a job – where I worked for nine years and gained invaluable experience and lasting connections –

LESSON 17: SHOW UP

because of a phone call my sister Debbie received. She said, "Come with me to the meeting." I almost didn't go, but I chose to show up – and that job changed my life. It would be remiss of me here not to acknowledge that Debbie is my "work angel". I cannot count the number of times she has invited me to 'show up' with the result being work, new connections, and money! Debbie has mastered the art of showing up, and I am forever indebted to her for how she lives this lesson.

Sometimes, in the pursuit of a dream, we become overwhelmed by the 'bigness' of it. Often, the magnitude of the task stops us from taking that first step. Sometimes the first step is simply showing up. Life takes care of the details when you listen to its nudges. An invitation is one of life's tools to nudge us forward. Don't ignore the nudges. They become your destiny. Answer the phone. Buy the ticket. Get on the bus – you never know where the journey will take you. Sometimes, 'showing up' is also about being a cheerleader for your own life. Make your own needs a priority and act accordingly. It is hard to show up for others when you are not showing up for yourself!

Showing up defeats procrastination. When you take the first step you turn *impossible* into *possible* – just by taking action, any action, you will find yourself in a new place. When you show up, you 'unlock your inaction'.

SHOW UP - LOCKDOWN DAY 17

OK, this is a tough one. How do you show up during lockdown? Now is certainly not the time to accept the invitation or get on the bus. When I first started my Facebook posts, I purposefully left some of them for what was to be the last week of lockdown. At the time, 'show up' seemed a perfectly good lesson for us as we prepared to re-enter the world. Now, here we are, facing three more weeks of *not* showing up. "What could showing up mean for now?", I wondered to myself as I went to sleep. I trusted that my subconscious mind would provide some answers.

This morning, as I walked towards my Journey cards, I spotted another card deck that sits close by – and that usually goes unnoticed. And then I had the answer. Don Miguel Ruiz is the author of the book *The Four Agreements*.[45] Having read the book, I purchased the set of cards that accompany the book. This was the deck that my eye noticed this morning. Based on ancient Toltec wisdom, Ruiz presents the four agreements as a means to break free from rules that we did not necessarily choose for ourselves. By integrating the agreements into our lives, he suggests, we can find freedom.

The Four Agreements are:
- Be impeccable with your word
- Don't take anything personally
- Don't make assumptions
- Always do your best

How is that for a list of things to live by? (Read the book, it's worth it.) I believe that in the fourth agreement lies the key to 'showing up' in lockdown. This is what Ruiz says about "Always do your best":

> *Your best is going to change from moment to moment; it will be different when you are healthy as opposed to*

---

[45] Don Miguel Ruiz, *The Four Agreements: A Practical Guide to Personal Freedom (A Toltec Wisdom Book)*, Amber-Allen Publishing, 1997.

LESSON 17: SHOW UP

sick. Under any circumstance, simply do your best, and you will avoid self-judgement, self-abuse and regret.

The way that you 'show up' in lockdown is to do your best – the operative word here is 'your': not my best, not your partner's best, not society's best. You do *your* best. And the best part of 'your best' is that you get to decide what it is! As we all wake up to the reality of another three weeks,[46] the tendency to start getting hard on ourselves is going to creep in. Am I being a good enough worker at home? A good enough home-school teacher? A good enough mother or father? A good enough partner? The list goes on – with each of us having our own 'not good enough' story running. Let it go. You, like me, like all of us, simply have to show up to lockdown by knowing and giving yourself permission to believe that you are doing your best for now. And whatever your best is – it is good enough.

Today is a public holiday (or, rather, a 'private holiday' as my Facebook friend Felix Jackson wryly observed). Lighten up. Take it easy. Lockdown is a marathon, not a sprint. Replace your 'not good enough' beliefs with 'good enough' ones. Let 'good enough' be your best for now. It's hard enough to work it out without mentally beating yourself up. Show up to your lockdown life with a new belief: I'm doing my best!

---

[46] The extension of the South African lockdown had just been announced.

LESSON 18
LOWER YOUR BUCKET

> *The world is full of abundance and opportunity, but far too many people come to the fountain of life with a sieve instead of a tank car... a teaspoon instead of a steam shovel. They expect little and, as a result, they get little.*
>
> — BEN SWEETLAND

Today's lesson is best encapsulated in the following story by Rebecca Fine. Although I know that it is not historically true, it is a great story that, quite literally, changed my life. It is called *Afloat in a Sea of Abundance*.[47]

> *In the days of the mighty sailing ships, when brave souls voyaged into the unknown, dependent on the winds and their as-yet incomplete knowledge of geography and navigation, one of the greatest and most dangerous challenges was to traverse the area known as 'the doldrums'. Extending about 30 degrees on either side of the equator, the doldrums are subject to days, weeks, even months of no wind at all. After a long and difficult crossing from Europe to South America, lying becalmed in the doldrums – with no land in sight and with the ship's supply of fresh water*

---

47 www.getmotivation.com/prosperity/sea-abundance-rfine.htm

dwindling – was a terrible and life-threatening situation. And so it happened that at times a ship would fetch up off the coast of South America, out of sight of shore, fresh water supplies exhausted and death knocking at the door. Then, with what must have been the sweetest sound those sailors could ever have hoped for, the lookout would suddenly call out that a ship was approaching in the distance.

Once the ship was within hailing distance, the cry went up: 'Water! Give us water!' And the reply would come back, 'Lower your buckets over the side.' You see, although the sailors didn't know it, they were afloat in a virtual river of drinkable and life-sustaining water flowing from the mouth of the powerful Amazon River, which carries nearly 20 percent of all the earth's runoff water into the sea with such force that the fresh (or brackish but safe) water flows as far as 100 miles out into the Atlantic.

The sailors, dying of thirst, only THOUGHT they were experiencing lack. The REALITY was that they were afloat in a literal sea of abundance. Exactly what they needed was within their reach the whole time, but the APPEARANCE of scarcity and their BELIEF in that appearance threatened to overpower them.

They could have died – and many certainly did – believing in lack while surrounded by abundance.

I came across this apocryphal story while researching material for a course for entrepreneurs on their relationship with money. I incorporated it into the course

LESSON 18: LOWER YOUR BUCKET

– which I taught for a few years. Towards the middle of 2015, while teaching the course, I found myself saying to yet another group of entrepreneurs, "You have nothing to fear. Money is all around you. Just lower your buckets." Suddenly, in my mind's eye, I saw myself uttering these words in 2016 – a year later. And I had my epiphany: If I were still in employment a year later, teaching others that they had nothing to fear, I would be a complete fake. How could I, in good conscience, be telling others to embrace abundance thinking, while I was too scared to do it myself?

> **When you have an abundance mentality, you believe that there is more than enough – of everything – to go around.**

I resigned, and a few months later, I began lowering my bucket. I reached out to every human being I had ever encountered who had the possibility of using my services. And the response was – and continues to be – overwhelmingly positive. I had hidden myself in the security that a monthly pay cheque brings, knowing that what I wanted most in the world was to be my own boss. All I had to do was lower my bucket! My beliefs about my own self-worth, and my ability to generate an income for myself, had me trapped in a doldrums of my own making while all around me the water was, in fact, quite drinkable.

This is not a treatise about self-employment. I spent many happy years being an employee, and I reaped many rewards – intellectual, social and financial. But my soul was calling out for more. I wanted independence, and I wanted to rely on myself to generate income. I took the leap.

I use this story to teach entrepreneurs the concept of an abundance mentality. One can, of course, embrace abundance and still be employed. Abundance is a mentality. When you have an abundance mentality, you believe that there is more than enough – of everything – to go around. In contrast, when you have a scarcity mentality, you believe that there is never enough, resulting in feelings of fear and anxiety. A scarcity mindset is pessimistic and dark; an abundance mindset is optimistic and light. But this story is actually about more than that. It is about the power of beliefs and how our beliefs can keep us stuck. For many years, I did not believe I had it in me to work for myself. And then I chose to lower my bucket. I found the courage to say, "Yes to life". Very few people know that the original title of Viktor Frankl's book, *Man's Search for Meaning*, was: *To Nevertheless Say 'Yes' to Life: A Psychologist Experiences the Concentration Camps.*

Lowering your bucket is, in my view, about saying yes to life. I urge you to say yes to life. If there is something you really want in life, go for it. Don't let self-defeating or untrue beliefs stand in your way. Examine your beliefs about yourself, about others and about life, test them and, if they no longer serve you, let them go. Lower your bucket. Take courage from the courage of Frankl and the other Holocaust survivors who rebuilt their lives, and who continued to drink from life's waters.

You can lower your bucket in any situation; it is not just about experiencing lack when there is, in fact, abundance. It is also about looking, investigating, and 'testing the waters'. The sailors assumed that the water was undrinkable. They never actually investigated their view of 'reality'. Assumptions are truly 'termites'.[48] They destroy from within and are often invisible until it is too late.

We all create stories in our heads that are full of assumptions. These stories usually have little to do with reality and can cause a range of emotions. We then react to these stories, leaving the other person bewildered. Remember they can't read your mind! When you choose to check your assumptions – for example, by asking questions – you are lowering your bucket. Relationships are much improved when there is the space for each person to lower their bucket, when required. It is, essentially, a 'reality check'. I practise this wherever possible. When I wish to verify the story that I am telling myself, I lower my bucket by simply asking the other if I may 'check reality'. Lowering my bucket lets truth, authenticity and intimacy onto my ship.

LOWER YOUR BUCKET – LOCKDOWN DAY 18

This is not the time to say no to life. No matter how hard it may be, it is our duty to continue to say yes. Moreover, we need to find ways to lower our buckets. What this means is that we need to examine our beliefs, and we need to ask

---

[48] Henry Winkler (American actor, comedian, author, executive producer and director) is quoted as saying that "assumptions are the termites of relationships".

whether they are serving us. Are they true? Is the water *really* not drinkable? What are we doing to test the waters? What are we doing to rid ourselves of beliefs that are no longer true? What new beliefs do we need to embrace?

While Covid-19 may be with us for a long time, we will not be in lockdown forever. When we re-enter the world, it is going to look vastly different. Survival is going to require us to lower our buckets. Those who cannot lower their buckets are going to be in trouble. Days before lockdown, I met Lael for breakfast. Over breakfast, she uttered these words, which have echoed for me throughout lockdown, "We all need to have a Plan B." For me, having a Plan B is a combination of lowering my bucket and holding steadfastly to an abundance mentality. I refuse to believe that I will not be able to continue to earn a living. I will not give in to a belief that says, "You can't drink the water." I intend to continue to lower my bucket, and I intend to continue to drink the water!

Succumbing to limiting beliefs and buying into a doomsday scenario will become a self-fulfilling prophecy. We will create it if we don't each take responsibility for saying yes to life. In practice what this means, for me, is the following:

- I am the economy. We are all the economy. It may be shut down at the moment, but when it re-opens, I intend to continue making money. I will do this by having a Plan B, a Plan C, and a Plan D. What are yours?
- I will not give in to a scarcity mentality. I will continue to be generous and to look after the less fortunate wherever I can. I will not hoard my money for fear of it running out. I will not be reckless, but I will not succumb to fear either. Will you join me?

LESSON 18: LOWER YOUR BUCKET

- I will examine all the beliefs I had in 2019 BC, and embrace new beliefs which are needed to survive – and thrive – in 2020 AC. Old beliefs will not serve me, and neither will limiting beliefs. I will embrace empowering beliefs. How about you?

Use today's lesson to consider how you will lower your bucket post-lockdown and what new beliefs you need to embrace to do so. Trust in your abundant abilities to handle any situation, meet any challenge or achieve any goal. If you know someone who is in need of some 'good talk' with a professional, I will be more than happy to support them to embrace new beliefs (that's me lowering my bucket). Happy Lowering Your Bucket Day!

> *It did not really matter what we expected from life, but rather what life expected from us. We needed to stop asking about the meaning of life, and instead to think of ourselves as those who were being questioned by life – daily and hourly. Our answer must consist, not in talk and meditation, but in right action and in right conduct. Life ultimately means taking the responsibility to find the right answer to its problems and to fulfil the tasks which it constantly sets for each individual.* [49]
>
> — **VIKTOR FRANKL**

---

49 Viktor E Frankl, *Man's Search for Meaning*, page 77. Beacon Press, 1959.

LESSON 19
TRAVEL LIGHT

Angels can fly because they take themselves lightly.
— G. K. CHESTERTON

My mother once told me this story. Her father, Tevye – my grandfather, after whom I was named – was a poor shoemaker. He had a small hole-in-the-wall shop on the Main Road in Woodstock, Cape Town. My grandmother, Bobba Chanke, would take him lunch every day. She would cook and plate a hot lunch, wrap it in a tea-towel and trundle down the hill to make sure that her husband ate every day. She would walk back up the hill and, a few hours later, she would walk back down the hill to fetch his plate. My bobba was neither fit nor thin. The daily walk up and down the hill was no easy feat. What my mother shared with me was that when my bobba and my grandfather were having a disagreement or a fight, and she returned to fetch the plate, the food was left untouched – my grandfather would rather starve than eat her lovingly prepared food.

I never knew my grandfather – he died a year before I was born. I have no idea what motivated him not to eat the food. Pride? Anger? Revenge? Who knows? But here's the point of the story. In my relationship with my partner, when he and I used to fight, I would not eat his food either. When we were fighting, I was suddenly not hungry. Just like my grandfather – who I never even met – I would rather starve than eat food prepared by someone with whom I was angry.

Emotional baggage is a strange thing. We are born into history, much of which we will never know. But, as much as genes play a role in who we are and what we become, I believe that we are born into – and with – baggage. How can I behave like a grandfather I never met? I certainly never learned the behaviour from him. Are genes responsible for behaviour? Of course, on some level – mainly physical, in my opinion – genetics play a huge role. But, in the example of the story above, I think that something else is at play: baggage – unconscious history that influences us in a myriad of ways.

The story of my grandfather and his self-defeating punishment of my bobba woke me up in a strange way. On the one hand, it allowed me to 'excuse' my behaviour – I was not responsible. I was simply acting out an unconscious script bequeathed to me by history. On the other hand, and more importantly, I allowed myself to take full responsibility. Did I want to behave in this way? Did I really want to be that unconscious? Or did I want to break the pattern? The answer was a resounding "Yes!" After hearing this story, I chose to check that particular piece of baggage. I began to be grateful for my partner's food, and I ate it, whether we were fighting or not. I am

LESSON 19: TRAVEL LIGHT

not my grandfather; nor do I wish to be him. I am my own person – a combination of genes and history – but I am also a person with choices. And my choice is to travel light.

When taking a flight, you are offered to have your baggage checked in. I am always surprised by how many people board a flight with all their luggage. Yes, it is easier on the other side not to have to wait for your suitcase, but the schlep factor that is involved in carrying both your hand luggage and your suitcase – and then wheeling it down the narrow aisle and forcing it into an overhead cabin – strikes me as a beautiful metaphor for life. You can *choose* to check in your luggage and then hand it over and allow it to disappear into the ether of the baggage handlers. You do not have to carry it all – you can simply travel with your hand luggage.

Travelling light requires you to become conscious of your behaviour, and to begin asking yourself a simple question: "Is this behaviour serving me positively?" Is it serving me to go to bed hungry? Of course not. So, there you go. Eat the food. Break the pattern. Is my resentment of my father serving me? Twenty years after he died? No. Right, let it go. Meditate. Go for therapy. Read books. Do whatever is required to stop the self-destructive behaviour. Wherever it may come from, be it genes or history, you can stop if you want to – but only once you recognise that it is not serving you.

Of course, behaviour is sometimes a result of chemicals and hormones. But that too can be treated. If medication is required, there is no need to suffer. Take the pill, work through the stuff, and heal yourself. Do it sooner rather than later. Heavy baggage causes pain – literally. Put it down if it is not something you need to travel with. The key to travelling light is forgiveness – which I touched on in **Lesson 2 (Monday Before Tuesday)**. Here we are talking about something more profound – not allowing Sunday to interfere too much with Monday, and 'Sunday' representing the stuff *back there*. That is really what baggage is – the stuff you bring from your past into the present.

> Do your work. Open your hand, open your heart, and let it go.

If you are being held back in the present from living your ultimate life, the chances are that a forgiveness process is required. Sometimes, it is ancestors who need forgiveness; at other times, it is people in your current life. And, of course, sometimes it is *you* who needs to forgive yourself. Either way, forgiveness is truly the panacea.

Often, when working with clients and suggesting that forgiveness may be in order, they look at me as if I'm crazy. "How?" they ask. They have held onto their resentments for so long that they find it almost impossible even to imagine the possibility of letting them go. I don't have an easy answer to the question – and I am in deep empathy with people who have been seriously scarred by others –

LESSON 19: TRAVEL LIGHT

but still, I urge forgiveness. Not for the person requiring the benefit of forgiveness, but for the person needing to forgive. To paraphrase the Buddha, resentment is like holding onto a hot coal and hoping the other person gets burned! When faced with a client who is struggling to let go and forgive, I have them make a tight fist. I then ask them to slowly open their hand – that is what forgiveness requires. Do your work. Open your hand, open your heart, and let it go.

TRAVEL LIGHT – LOCKDOWN DAY 19

In **Lesson 13 (Choose Again)**, I mentioned a friend to whom I needed to apologise, and from whom I wanted to ask forgiveness. Two days after writing the post, I phoned Belinda, apologised, and we moved on. I have used this time to forgive myself for past transgressions, I have had old friends reconnect with me, and I have asked for forgiveness from some. I have shed some of the baggage that I have been schlepping around. While, like many of us, I may be packing on the kilos, I am losing the weight of the baggage. For me, the baggage comes from BC Time. Why would I want to schlep it into AC Time? There will be enough to deal with there.

Travel Light has another meaning – one that I discovered after writing the original book. Its meaning could well be another lesson – but I have committed to 22 Lessons, so indulge me as I connect the lesson to travelling light. The lesson is "Find the Funny".

One of the joys of this time has been the hilarious memes and clips that have emerged. Some of them have literally had me belly-laughing. You cannot travel light without a sense of humour. And a sense of humour is key to getting through the hard times.

Viktor Frankl said (slightly paraphrased):

> *An outsider to the camps would be astonished to hear that one could find a sense of humour there as well; of course, only the faint trace of one, and then only for a few seconds or minutes.* [50]

Even in the direst of circumstances, inmates could find a semblance of humour. It may have been dark humour – the humour of the desperate – but it helped.

> **Ask yourself a simple question: "Is this behaviour serving me positively?"**

Humour is, according to Frankl, one of the soul's weapons in the fight for self-preservation. I love that phrase "the soul's weapon". The attempt to develop a sense of humour and see things in a humorous light is, according to Frankl: "some kind of a trick learned while mastering the art of living. Humour has an ability to rise above any situation, even for only for a few seconds." So, yes, it is serious – and there is a lot to be concerned about. But – and I say this with utter humility and respect – if

---

50 Viktor E Frankl, *Man's Search for Meaning*, page 46. Beacon Press, 1959.

LESSON 19: TRAVEL LIGHT

Frankl and his fellow inmates could find ways, albeit dark, to find a little bit of funny in their dire circumstances, who are we not to do the same?

As I read yesterday, "Do you know what the biggest waste of money has been so far?" … "A fucking 2020 Diary". I hope you find a bit of funny today. Wherever possible, travel light, my fellow AC travellers.

My favourite clip of all time is found here:
www.youtube.com/watch?v=Ow0lr63y4Mw.

If you are reading this offline, Google 'Bob Newhart Psychologist' to watch the clip. Not only is it hilarious, but it also has tongue-in-cheek relevance to today's lesson.

LESSON 20
DROP THE COMPARISON

The reason why we struggle with insecurity is because we compare our behind the scenes with everyone else's highlight reel.
— STEVEN FURTICK

I was not a happy child. My father was too old. I wanted a younger father – like my friends' fathers. My home was a hotel. I wanted a house in the suburbs, with a pool, like my friends' houses. I wanted to be taller. I wanted a deeper voice. I wanted to like the girls, not the boys. I wanted everything that others had. I did not want what I had. Comparing myself to others became my modus operandi for life. Then I grew up and I looked back at all the wasted time. My father died, and only then did I appreciate all the gifts he had given me. My childhood home was perfect. Who gets to say they grew up in a residential hotel? The stories and the lessons have not only shaped me; they have served me. I wasted so much time wishing for reality to be different. Imagine that.

When we compare ourselves with others, we are essentially fighting life. That's a fight you cannot win. But dropping the comparison is not about losing one's aspirations for better, different, or more. I'd love to be as disciplined and driven as the toned athlete at the gym.

If I look at the athlete and beat myself up for not being enough, rather than aspiring to be like him, then the comparison is a self-defeating one. When I look at the athlete and admire him, using his example to motivate me, then I am not engaging in comparison. Comparison, when it is used to belittle yourself (or others for that matter) is a dangerous practice. These thoughts do not motivate. "I am not enough" is not a driver of positive behaviour. It is a driver of staying stuck.

Social media has made this lesson even harder for us. We are bombarded with images of perfect bodies and perfect lives – forgetting that we are only seeing the 'highlights reel'. Instead, we scroll some more and feed ourselves subconscious messages of endless comparisons – scrolling through your social media feed is not action! When you spend your life wishing for things to be different, but taking little action to change, you are basically addicted to comparison. Comparing yourself and your circumstances to others is essentially just noise in your head. You need to consciously tune it out, or, as a former colleague says, "turn down the volume". When you lower the volume of the voice that is saying, "I wish I were like him" or "I wish I had what she has", you free up space in your head to plan, set goals, and take action, not from a place of "*I'm not enough*", but from a place of "*I want something different*". That is a completely different motivator!

You are unique. That is the bottom line. Why would you choose not to celebrate your uniqueness? At the very same moment that I am wishing to be like the athlete, he is wishing to be more like someone else, who is probably also wishing to be buffer, fitter, thinner, and so on. There will always be someone with more, just as there will always be someone with less. You are perfect as you are. When you recognise your innate perfection and come from a place of "*I am enough*", you allow yourself to become more. Brandon Bays has, in my opinion, captured the essence of this message in her card called 'Perfection'. This is what she says:

> *There is an innate perfection that pervades all of Life. The rosebud is as complete in its perfection as the rose in full bloom. That same perfection is in the faded rose petals and even in the decayed petals as they offer themselves back to the soil.*

And then she ends with my favourite line of all time:

God does not need your help to make Life more perfect.

Although these words are not expressed specifically in the context of comparisons, they state, in my opinion, the essence of the belief required to drop the comparisons, once and for all. You *are* enough! You *are* perfect in your imperfection. You *are* where you need to be, and life is unfolding as it should be. Do you want to change? Great! Do you want more? Go for it! But be the rosebud on its way to becoming the rose. The rosebud does not say to itself, "*I wish I were a rose*". It is perfectly content to be the rosebud. Little does it know that simply by doing what rosebuds do, it is on its way to becoming a rose.

Of course, human beings have agency in a way that plants do not. But using that agency to compare yourself with others just wastes your time. Use your agency not only to relish being a rosebud, but also to do what needs doing to *become* a rose. Don't reject your rosebud stage.

Do it by aspiring to become the rose if that is what you want to become. Not only will you enjoy the journey more; you will also be a much prettier rose. But then, who's comparing? You will be the rose you need to be, thorns and all.

Everyone has their own journey to walk. There is no one way to do things, and no one person who can be used as a measure or baseline for anything. Focusing on other people, instead of working towards achieving your own goals, will leave you feeling frustrated and hopeless.

> When you recognise your innate perfection and come from a place of "I am enough", you allow yourself to become more.

DROP THE COMPARISON – LOCKDOWN DAY 20

Midnight tonight marks the end of Day Twenty. We thought this would be a three-week thing. And here we are with another fourteen days to go. Or not. Who knows? If ever there was a time to accept reality as it is, this is it. No amount of resistance is going to help us here. We are required to accept that we happen to be alive during the Great Plague of 2020. Twenty years from now, children will write essays on us.

LESSON 20: DROP THE COMPARISON

I have, in numerous points, emphasised the importance of acceptance, not only of reality but also of ourselves. Today's lesson lends itself to a spelling out of the imperative: Acceptance is key; Resistance is futile. Some people resist acceptance, thinking that acceptance is passive, a giving up of sorts. But it is not.

As Mindy Diamond says:

> *Acceptance is the most powerful stance in the world. Acceptance says: 'I recognise that this is my reality and I am in charge of how I want to live my life. It is within my power and purview to impact my life and, if I accept my circumstances as they are, I am actively choosing to do so.* [51]

Acceptance is not failure, resignation or apathy. Acceptance is the beginning. When we drop the comparison, we move into a space of acceptance. I have used this time to do some serious soul-searching with regards to what needs acceptance in my life. I am ashamed to say that, for an exceedingly long time, I have been one of those people who goes to the gym to clock in. I swipe my card and turn around. I don't want to lose my discount fee, and one day I'll start gymming properly. Bullshit. Just before lockdown, I cancelled my membership. I'm fifty-one years old. I hate gym. Who am I kidding? I'm not saying I won't exercise. It's just not going to happen in that form and at that place. I'm tired of lying to myself. Lockdown is Acceptance Time. From a place of quiet acceptance, I will make my changes, but not from a place of comparison and not from a place of

---

[51] www.thriveglobal.com

denial. Comparison and Denial were my BC states. I want to find new AC states of being, doing and having.

Today my website went live. I have procrastinated for four years on getting it done. One of the main reasons was that I did not believe I had 'enough' for a website – certainly not compared to 'real' businesses, to 'real' writers, to 'real' therapists, and so on. Then, I dropped the comparison. My business is the size it is. I am the writer I am. I am the therapist I am. All enough. All good enough. If I cannot make peace with what is now, I never will. From that place, I can make all the changes I deem necessary.

I think that it is a cop-out not to get started on things because of lockdown. We may not be able to go anywhere, but this is the time to press "play". For those of us old enough to remember video machines, when we pressed "pause", the screen would flicker. Many of us, myself included, have had things in our life on "pause". I often encourage clients with the words, "press play". Very often, we are in pause mode because we haven't dropped the comparison. When you stop comparing yourself to others, you simultaneously get on with the business of pressing play. You accept what needs accepting and, from that place, you start your journey of change.

I spent a lot of BC Time on pause. In December 2019 BC, I ended my twenty-year relationship with Kevin. I made a very painful choice when I pressed "play" on a new life. Many of the lessons I have shared were learned in the context of a very deep and meaningful relationship with him. My debt of gratitude to him, for the life we shared, and for the lessons, is enormous. I will also use this opportunity, in keeping with the spirit of previous

LESSON 20: DROP THE COMPARISON

lessons, to apologise and ask forgiveness for all the hurt I caused. I want to use this post to tell the truth faster and play in the light.

A friend of mine wrote the following words in an e-mail the other day in response to a post: "As much truth as we tell, it is shrouded in words that cannot express the reality of our lives."

I love that sentence. It holds so much wisdom. I have spent this lockdown in a cottage on my own. I love my cottage, and I *really* am having a positive lockdown experience. At the same time, I am deeply aware of, and reflective on, the choices I have made. So, when I say, "press play", it is from a deep place of knowing that we can never predict how the movie will continue once we press play. What I do know for sure is that my movie is *my* movie. Your movie is *your* movie. Comparing my movie to your movie is futile. But, most importantly, as the quote that introduces this piece reminds us, don't compare your 'behind the scenes' with other's highlight reels. Backstage is always messy. Our lives are messy. Covid-19 is making them even messier. It's okay. We're all living messy lives. Make peace with yours. Change what needs changing. Just drop the comparison.

LESSON

21

BREATHE

I took a deep breath and listened to the old brag of my heart. I am, I am, I am.

— SYLVIA PLATH *(The Bell Jar)*

I have struggled with smoking for most of my adult life. What started as an attempt to look cool turned into a crutch, a habit, and then an addiction. Mark Twain is credited with saying, "Giving up smoking is the easiest thing in the world. I know because I've done it thousands of times." At least I'm in good company. [52]

Smoking – starting, stopping, and re-stopping – has made me acutely aware of something we take for granted most of the time – our breath. Breath is quite literally God's gift to us. No breath; no life – it is as simple as that. In Genesis, man is created when God breathes into him:

> *The Lord God formed the man from the dust of the ground and breathed into his nostrils the breath of life, and the man became a living being.*
>
> — GENESIS 2:7

Some translations say that man became "a living soul". The Creation story may be a myth but, like all myths, it comes to illuminate some powerful life lessons. The Hebrew word for 'breath' is *neshama*, which also means

---

[52] I am happy to report that, as of October 2022, I have been cigarette-free for 6 weeks!

soul. Breath, therefore, is not just a physical thing – it has a spiritual dimension. Many other ancient languages use the same word for air, wind or breath as they do for life, vital energy or spirit. This spirit of life is called chi, ki, prana or energy. When you breathe you are connecting not just to your physical body, but to something much deeper – you are connecting to your soul.

One more Biblical reference: in the *Songs of Solomon*, we read that "breath restores me to my exact self." This line expresses the importance of breathing, and the connection between our breath and our essential self – or 'exact self' as the Bible has it – beautifully. I am talking about a specific breath here – generally, we breathe without thinking about it. There is another breath that we call 'conscious breathing'.

> If you want to live a truly spiritual life, then conscious breathing is your tool.

Conscious breathing is a built-in anti-anxiety tool, given to us by life – or God, depending on your view. Life has given us a method to deal with stress and anxiety. Try it right now. Breathe in deeply through your nose, hold it for a few seconds and then breathe out through your mouth. Try it a few times. It is almost impossible not to

LESSON 21: BREATHE

relax slightly when we breathe consciously. Breath is the doorway to your essence. When you breathe consciously, you allow yourself to be fully present in the moment. Conscious breathing – in through your nose and out through your mouth – clears your mind and focuses you on the task at hand. If you want to live a truly spiritual life – a life in which you are not continuously swayed by whatever life is throwing your way – then conscious breathing is your tool. Breathing is the language of the soul.[53]

Dan Brulé (Guchu Ram Singh) is a world-renowned leader in the Spiritual Breathing Movement. This is what he has to say about conscious breathing – which he calls *Spiritual Breathing*. I am quoting from this Master extensively, as I could not say it better myself:

> *Spiritual Breathing can take you to the eye of the storms in your life. Spiritual breathing can help you to balance yin and yang, peace and power, rhythm, and harmony. Learn from the breath itself. Follow your own bliss!" Start by watching your breath. Do what the Buddha did at the moment of enlightenment: follow the breath as it comes and goes. Feel the sensations of breath, the movement of breath in you. Be a witness. Observe, notice, pay attention to what is happening inside of you in each moment, and be aware of the one being aware! Add to that the willingness to let go, to surrender. And then begin to conspire with the life that surrounds and permeates everything in existence. Breathe consciously. Feel the expansion and contraction of life! Celebrate the flow*

---

53 Adapted from www.breathmastery.com

of life, and marvel at the mysteries that life reveals to you through the breath. Seek out others who are committed to breath mastery. Share your experience – breathe peace and love, freedom and safety, energy and aliveness, love and light, and watch the world within you and around you change forever. [54]

Slow and steady breaths send a message to your brain that all is well. In so doing, they calm your mind down. Replace overthinking and anxiety with conscious breathing. It works!

> Slow and steady breaths send a message to your brain that all is well.

BREATHE – LOCKDOWN DAY 21

Followers of my posts will have noticed that many of my lessons contain the directive to breathe. Keep breathing. Today, I am adding "conscious" to the directive. Don't just breathe – breathe consciously. This tiny action makes the difference between calm or stress; response or reaction; discussion or fighting. Breathe consciously and breathe deeply. Often. I was speaking to my friend, Anne Trusler, last night. She is spending lockdown with her children

---

54 Dan Brulé, *Just Breathe: Mastering Breathwork*, Atria/Enliven Books, 2017.

LESSON 21: BREATHE

and grandchildren in a beautiful area of South Africa. She told me that she doesn't use the word 'lockdown'. She prefers the word 'sanctuary'. How beautiful is that? For her, and for those of us fortunate enough to have access to resources and space, there is something peaceful about this time. We have time and space to breathe. Conscious breathing takes us inside, away from the noise. It is a way for us to connect to the deepest part of ourselves, to create sanctuary moments for ourselves.

Eckhart Tolle said, "If you get the inside right, the outside will fall into place." [55] Now, where we have so little control over the outside, conscious breathing is a way to get the inside right. When you learn to control your breath, you learn to control your emotions and responses. You become calm, clearheaded and focused – no matter what is happening in the external world. We need, now – more than ever – to find ways to quiet our minds. If you have a way to be alone, some form of daily meditation – basically, conscious breathing – is highly recommended. The trick to meditating is simply to breathe consciously and let each thought just come and go, come and go, and come and go. Don't follow the thoughts; rather watch them as you would watch the traffic passing you by. Don't follow the cars. Let them speed away, and keep breathing deeply. [56]

---

[55] Eckhart Tolle, *The Power of Now: A Guide to Spiritual Enlightenment*, Namaste Publishing, 1997.

[56] Thanks to Stefan Brozin for that one.

LESSON 22
YAY ME!

*The more you praise and celebrate your life,
the more there is in life to celebrate.*
— OPRAH WINFREY

I was reading a story to a five-year-old child who is very close to my heart. Lying on her bed – her head on my shoulder – she was looking at the pictures when suddenly, she let out a fart. She looked up at me and, without hesitation, uttered the magical words: "Yay Me!" We both burst out laughing. I continued reading, but that moment is indelibly etched in my mind, as are the words she used – *Yay Me!* These words are the epitome of self-acceptance. And self-acceptance is, in my opinion, the key to a life well lived.

Self-acceptance is not self-resignation – it is not an excuse for not changing. In fact, the opposite is true. Action is key. People confuse acceptance with complacency. But it is not about being complacent – it's about taking action and making changes from a place of acceptance, rather than from a place of beating yourself up. When you accept yourself – warts and all – you also accept what requires changing. Coming from a place of self-acceptance, you do not beat yourself up for what you are *not* – you embrace your positive, and you accept the negative, in order to begin changing what needs changing.

Yay Me! says, "This is me. This is who I am. This is how I am." *Yay Me!* allows you to look in the mirror with a benevolent eye – with kindness, and with love. *Yay Me!* celebrates the self – it acknowledges that we are not human beings, but humans *being* – humans being good; humans being bad; humans being happy; humans being sad; humans succeeding; and humans failing. *Yay Me!* liberates you. *Yay Me!* accepts you and opens up the possibility to accept others. Imagine living in a world where *Yay Me!* was an acceptable expression of appreciation for yourself and *Yay You!* an expression of gratitude towards others.

I believe that the world would be a better place if, instead of asking, "What's wrong?", we asked, "What's right?" We are hard-wired, and then conditioned, for negativity – for seeing what's wrong, what's absent and what's missing. We share the bad news but keep the good news to ourselves. When I ghost write, I often have to ask my clients please to tell me what is good about the work before they point out the problems. It is as if we take the good for granted, and focus on the negative. How often does a teacher phone a parent to tell them how wonderful their child is? No, the teacher phones when the child has been naughty, or when the child is struggling.

A wise teacher, Moshe Caspi – who helped me to frame my own philosophy of education – once posed the following question: "Why do we give children extra lessons in what they are bad at?" Indeed, we should have extra lessons in what we are good at! This is the essence of *Yay Me!* Celebrate what is good, beautiful and true

LESSON 22: YAY ME!

about yourself – focus there. There will always be stuff that needs changing, and stuff that needs work. Attend to those things, but attend to them from a *Yay Me!* place. Live your life in celebration of self and others. Live a *Yay Me!* life.

> Live your life in celebration of self and others. Live a YAY ME! life.

YAY ME! - LOCKDOWN DAY 22 AND BEYOND

Lesson 22. We made it! Look at us – survivors, one and all.

Today's post is a very personal one, written to all the people who have journeyed with me for the past twenty-two days. I did it, and your love and support has touched me deeply. Old friends have become new friends. New friends have become old friends. My gratitude is enormous. I have learned so many lessons through these lessons – and from you. I did not present the lessons in their original order. I allowed life to lead the way. Each day a phone call, or text, or e-mail would lead me to the next lesson. Writing these daily posts has been the biggest TTP of my life. It has, in fact, been an exercise in living – and sometimes failing at – all the lessons: Monday before Tuesday, Live in the light, Be grateful, Make it up as you go along … the list goes on. What a gift to learn, relearn and unlearn from your life lessons.

My niece, the muse of this book, did her final matric art project on the concept of 'liminal space'. I confessed to her that I had never heard of it. As she explained it to me, the teacher became the pupil. A liminal space is a waiting area between one point and another. My favourite liminal space is literally a waiting area – it is the Duty-Free area of airports. I take "duty-free" quite literally. I'm packed, through passport control, and a new adventure awaits. Liminal spaces are transitional and transformative. They have an expectancy about them – escalators, hotel corridors late at night, and empty parking lots. Liminal spaces are not always physical – divorce, job loss, and moving, for example. We can add lockdown to that list.

> *Liminality is as much a state of the human mind as it is a particular place.* [57]

A rite of passage is a liminal state when we stand on the threshold between two different states of being. Lockdown has been, for me, and – I suspect – for you, a real "going inside" experience. That is what makes it liminal. When you arrive on the other side of a liminal space, a shift must have occurred.

Disruption, the clarion call of our generation, has become a self-fulfilling prophecy. It may get a lot worse before it gets better. Make peace with it. We are living in unprecedented times where there is no rule book. Each of us, individually, needs to dig deep, steel ourselves, and find new ways of being and doing this human thing.

Yesterday, I had an informal coaching session with a former colleague, Andrew Stead. He has followed the

---

[57] www.betterhelp.com

posts and been supportive throughout, and I am grateful to him. We discussed the challenges of lockdown, particularly for the self-employed. Our discussion helped me to distil a list of "take-aways":

My ten guiding beliefs for life now

1. It is unfolding as it is supposed to.
2. You are an entrepreneur – or can be one if needs be.
3. Focus where necessary. Diversify where necessary.
4. Notice the "before Covid" thoughts when they arise. Welcome them, and then let them go.
5. Replace the "before Covid" thoughts with new thoughts: I trust, I am looked after, I can make money.
6. Make data-driven decisions as opposed to fear-based ones.
7. Eliminate fear as much as possible. Replace it with trust (breathe fear out; breathe trust in).
8. Money needs to move – that is why it's called cash flow.
9. Go easy on yourself. The unknown is always scary. Change is a slow and gradual process.
10. Let go of the outcome completely. The journey, not the goal, is the point.

I will be using these ten new beliefs to create a *Yay Me!* life. I hope and trust that you will use some of these and add your own. Either way, *Yay You!*

TWENTY-TWO LESSONS FOR NOW

A GUIDE TO CRAFTING A LIFE OF MEANING AND JOY

AFTERWORD

It is risky to write about a historical moment while the events are underway. Even now, two years since the first lockdown, the narrative continues to unfold in unpredictable ways. There is no way of knowing how events will turn out. My recipe is simple: stay in the now, let your eyes gaze softly towards the future, remain unattached to the outcome, and find meaning in the moment.

Deal with what comes, as it comes.

I have sometimes joked that this book could be published posthumously – because that is how uncertain the future is. Worrying about it is truly a waste of imagination.

If you find yourself reading this book at a time when events have overtaken some of the views expressed, that is okay. I let go of the need to be "right" a long time ago. The present time is the longest experiment in being consciously aware of how little we "know" that I have ever encountered. Certainty has always been an illusion, and uncertainty is now the ordained order of the day. The sooner we make peace with this, the better our physical, mental and emotional health will be. And if uncertainty is the way it is – all the more reason to take it one day at a time. I will continue to pray, stay grateful, and give each day my best. I trust you will be able to do the same. I wish us all health, happiness, and love. Life is so much better with these three gifts.

This version of the book, that you are about to finish, is the third edition. The journey of working on this book and the gifts that it continues to bring to my life are immeasurable. I would need a new book to thank everyone who has supported me on this journey. I trust that I have expressed my gratitude to all of you. As part of the unfolding, my friend – and wonderful graphic designer – Bradley Kirshenbaum created the graphics for each lesson. They will become printed cards. I, and all the people who have supported me on this journey, am using the lessons to guide us. We trust the process, make it up as we go along, and keep lowering our buckets. As this book is going to print, a Zulu version of the cards is being finalised. From there, we will move to the next language. Who knows where these will take me? I am unattached to the outcome.

> Stay in the now, let your eyes gaze softly towards the future, remain unattached to the outcome, and find meaning in the moment. Deal with what comes, as it comes.

AFTERWORD

'Finding yourself' is not really how it works. You aren't a ten-dollar bill in last winter's coat pocket. You are also not lost. Your true self is right there, buried under cultural conditioning, other people's opinions, and inaccurate conclusions you drew as a kid that became your beliefs about who you are. 'Finding yourself' is actually returning to yourself. An unlearning, an excavation, a remembering who you were before the world got its hands on you. [58]

— EMILY MCDOWELL

---

[58] www.emandfriends.com/products/finding-yourself-card

www.ingramcontent.com/pod-product-compliance
Lightning Source LLC
Chambersburg PA
CBHW022014290426
44109CB00015B/1169